Tedward

CARYL PEARSON

Outskirts Press, Inc.
http://www.outskirtspress.com

ISBN: 978-1-4787-3922-7

Outskirts Press and the "OP" logo are trademarks belonging to Outskirts Press, Inc.

PRINTED IN THE UNITED STATES OF AMERICA

outskirtspress
DENVER, COLORADO

Caryl and Joe at Foothills Ranch, April, 1974, about a month before heading up to Estes Park to start their first trail guiding job. That is the horseshoer's blue pickup. He was fond of Joe, and it was he that discovered that Joe knew how to "shake hands", and also that he was "broke to drive". He used to say "That old nag of yours is smarter than a shithouse rat."

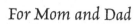
For Mom and Dad

This is a collection of stories that I have loved to tell and re-tell over the years. I finally decided to write them down, just in case I out-live my wits. Someone asked me once if I've ever craved "fame and fortune". That would be a yes. But the main reason I wrote this book is so these memories wouldn't be lost.

If you love the outdoors, wildlife, horses, and working with others that do, this job—being a wrangler and trail guide in beautiful country—is for you. And the icing on the cake? Getting to share your love of it all with hundreds of people that have never experienced it in the particular way that you are going to show it to them. You are fostering love and appreciation for this planet and its creatures, terrain, weather, and all its wonders, and you are having one hell of a good time doing it.

This is a true story. No names were
changed to protect the innocent—
or the guilty.

Tedward

Chapter 1

He came from Greeley, Colorado, where my friend Susan found him wandering alone at a very tender age. She scooped him up and brought him to me in the mountains of Estes Park, where I shared a cabin and 2 ½ acres with Nikki, my Siberian Husky, Joe, my Quarter Horse, and Chuck, my tabby cat. I wasn't too keen on having another dog, but I agreed to look after him until I could find him a good home. Hah—famous last words. By the time someone suitable came along, I realized I couldn't part with him.

Sue called him "Little Pud". I called him Teddy, because he did sort of resemble a tiny bear cub. But it was my old trail-guiding buddy Chris who gave him the name that stuck: Tedward. "Why "Tedward"?", I asked him, and he answered, "I don't know—he's just so Tedward in his ways!"

His amusing antics soon had us captivated. The jaunty way he would trot into a room, assuming everything in it was his to command, or the way he would bite Nikki's elbows from underneath her belly—perhaps getting even from the tramplings he endured in the yard—he had presence, and he was a natural entertainer. Soon after he arrived, we had an influx of large dogs whose owners were going on vacation. So in addition to Nikki, Tedward, and Sue's shepherd-husky mix Bean, we had Spirit, a Newfoundland mix, Tasha and Tim, both purebred Siberians, and Rocky, a beefy Irish Setter cross. It wasn't long before they were all running around the yard, sometimes with my horse Joe joining in. Tedward was electrified by this, and would sit by the porch, trembling and whining. He soon learned not to venture out in the open when the galloping was going on, because Nikki would make a beeline for him and flat-out mow him down. He'd tumble over and ki-yi his way back to the safety of the porch steps.

But he got his revenge in the evening, when all the adult dogs would be worn out from a long day of wrestling and cavorting, and would sprawl out all over the living room floor, looking like some weird lumpy carpet. Tedward would step to the doorway, look over the scene, and select his first victim. Tail-chewing, ear-pulling, leg-grabbing mayhem ensued, accompanied by vicious snarls and growls, until his target was so enraged he or she would leap up, roaring, aiming to teach the little upstart a lesson. Tedward would dart under the nearest chair, eyes agleam with mischief. The dogs were better entertainment than TV could ever be—and it was live!

When Tedward got a few months older and could run faster, Nikki would lead him on merry chases through the trees and across the open spaces in our yard, staying just out of his reach. This so infuriated Tedward that he would make a loud roaring sound, sort of like a hound's bay, but rougher and lower-pitched. Nikki would cut so close to the tree trunks that in the heat of the chase, Tedward would sometimes miscalculate and run right into one. Nikki seemed to have a satisfied look on her face, her tongue lolling as she watched him stagger around, dazed after one of these collisions.

Tedward didn't seem to mind being dressed up and made to sit on the couch for pictures, perhaps because he was still young enough to consider it just a normal part of life. He was truly a natural "party animal", as he always seemed up for any activity that involved lots of humans and dogs and other critters—his motto would've been, then and always, "the more, the merrier." One thing he didn't like was horseback riding. I believe he was vastly relieved when around age 5 months I stopped slinging him over the saddle in front of me, and let him run alongside. He was interested in wild animals, but he didn't have Nikki's killer instinct. The funny thing was, it seemed that the creatures could sense this, because I noticed that he could sometimes get pretty close to deer, rabbits, mice and birds.

In July of 1976, when he was about 6 months old, I took Tedward on his first overnight wilderness family jaunt, with Nikki and Joe. We went up the Meadow Mountain Trail near Allenspark, Colorado—I was interested to see how far up we could get, as there was still quite a bit of snow in the high country. I was hoping Nikki wouldn't teach him any of her walkabout tricks, such as disappearing for hours at a time and showing up farther along the trail, after I'd bitten my fingernails to the quick, wondering where she was. Both dogs were pretty good the first day, mostly following close behind Joe on the sometimes-narrow mountain trail. As the sun dropped behind Mt. Alice, I chose a charming little meadow to camp in for the night. I strung a tube tent between 2 aspens, in case of a shower, but put down my pad and down bag by the stream that ran through the middle of the meadow. I tethered Joe to a sturdy tree, and he immediately began munching the luscious grass. I allowed the dogs to explore the area while I built a campfire in the stone ring and started making dinner. To this day, on camping trips I still feed my dogs Kibbles and Bits and weenies and cheese—no picky eaters with that menu. For me, macaroni and cheese and instant coffee, with a Snickers bar for dessert. Wouldn't want to totally lose touch with civilization. After enjoying our dinner and the sunset and the lovely piney smell of our campsite, it was time to get cozy in my sleeping bag. Tedward curled up right by my shoulder, while Nikki was lying a short distance away, sniffing the evening air. I drifted off to sleep thinking to myself, this is the life.

Some time later, I awoke to the sound of muffled yelps and crashing bushes. I heard Joe's hooves beat the ground briefly as he startled, and Tedward leaped up as I struggled out of my bag and ran toward the sound. There was no moon, but the starlight was bright enough for me to glimpse a leaping, twirling form that had to be Nikki. I lunged and caught her by the collar, feeling something sharp prick my hand. When I got the flashlight beam on her, what a sight it was—her face and neck were covered with dozens of porcupine quills!

The actual count was 73. It took me an hour and a half to pull them out, with Nikki trapped between my knees, not having fun, and Tedward looking on. Luckily I had scissors and pliers in my pack; in those days it was thought that if you snipped the top of the quill, it would break the vacuum and make the quill easier to pull out. After that ordeal, I figured she'd learned her lesson and wouldn't try attacking the porcupine again, so I left her untied. I know, I know—what a dufus-brain. I'm sure you can guess what happened. As I once again snuggled down into the luxurious comfort of my down bag, with my chastened husky curled up next to me, I had images in my mind of the delicious bacon and eggs I was going to cook over the campfire in the morning. But there was to be another interruption before then.

After another timeless interval of peaceful sleep, we were again awakened by odd noises coming from the brushy area to the south. This time Nikki came barreling towards us before I could get out of my bag, and skidded to a halt snorting and sneezing and pawing at her face . Yes, there were quills, but—not nearly as many. We went through the same procedure as before, while I admonished her in no uncertain terms that if she ever wanted to be free on a camping trip again, there was to be no more harassing the wildlife.

I can hear the cries of, "Idiot!", "Lamebrain!", etc. now: I did not tie her up. The sky was just beginning to show light when I felt a nudge on my cheek. There was Her Highness, with a mere smattering of quills on her neck and flank. Either she was wising up or there was one bald porcupine wandering around. Tedward was observing all this and apparently learning something, because in his entire life of 15 years, much of it spent in wild areas, he never got one quill.*

We only had Nikki with us for 2 years. I was in southern California with both dogs in January of 1977, getting ready to take the train up north to volunteer at the California Marine Mammal Center. I had a wooden traveling crate for Nikki and a plastic one for Tedward. I was sitting in my seat and a conductor came up and asked me if I was the one with the dogs, and when I said yes, and he said, "Come with me", I got a sinking feeling in my stomach. When we got off the train and back to the baggage car, there was Nikki's crate in pieces on the ground, and no dog in sight. They said the crate had been dropped, and "the dog ran off."

Thus began one of the worst weeks of my life. I let Tedward and my baggage go on to San Francisco, and spent 7 miserable days trying to find Nikki. No dice. She was pretty shy with strangers; I can only hope that she made it to the Santa Monica Mountains where just maybe she could fend for herself, given her talent for catching small critters. I recalled how she allowed slack in her chain, when we were visiting a ranch in Lyons, Colorado, and waited perfectly still, watching as the clueless chickens quickly lost their awareness of her proximity, and sprang and caught one when it wandered into range.

Other fond memories began coming to my mind, such as her penchant for stealing my purple mittens, and burying them in the snow in the yard. I would try spying on her, and if she caught me, she'd stop, dig up the mitten, and carry it somewhere out of my sight, looking furtively over her shoulder as she did so. Another favorite of hers was tormenting Joe when he was eating grain out of his feed tub. She'd do a "run-by", and try to nip his nose as she passed. Joe would lay his ears back and shake his head menacingly, one time even striking at her with a front hoof. She would also get very excited when she saw Joe rolling in the yard. I'm pretty sure that was her predator instinct, never far from the surface, telling her that any animal down and thrashing around could soon translate into "dinner is served."

She was strong for her size. At 45 pounds, she was capable of pulling me, at 110 lbs. (man, those were the days) on my cross-country skis. She was also beautiful, with a grey and white coat, and one eye blue and the other eye half-blue, half-brown.

It was at the Marine Mammal Center that it became really obvious that Tedward was at home with other species. In those days, there would sometimes be a young seal or sea lion loose in the building or on the grounds for a short period of time. Tedward never showed any aggression or fear around them, just a sort of polite interest and acceptance. But maybe this was because they didn't move too fast; I do recall a certain deer-chasing incident on the property.

He also developed a friendship with our pet rat, Moon. At first, when they were showing alot of interest in each other, I was a bit afraid to let them get together. I'd seen Tedward's hunting instinct triggered by other rodents, such as gophers and prairie dogs. He never caught one, but his chasing of them was awfully enthusiastic.

But then came a mellow summer afternoon when I was sitting with my feet up on the windowsill, enjoying the sight of the greenery in the yard and the pleasant feel of the breeze, with Moon running around exploring the room—and Tedward pushed the door open and strolled in. Instead of jumping up and grabbing the rat, I decided to stay relaxed and see what would happen. I'd been telling Tedward for weeks, "This is a pet, don't hurt her", and things of that sort. Lo and behold, they started to play. Tedward would look predatory, in his posture and expression, but he never harmed her. Moon was quite the mischievous little prankster, nipping his toes and dashing here and there. At one point Tedward actually pinned her to the floor with his mouth, Moon uttering some strident squeaks; I thought, this is it, he's having rat for lunch. But no—a second later, there she was unhurt (though soggy), going for his feet again. They played for 15 minutes without stopping.

My friend and housemate Holly saw and marveled at their antics later the same evening. Holly had a Lhasa Apso named Bandito, and at first, we kept hold of him when the other two were playing, just to be on the safe side. But before long, all 3 animals were cavorting all over our spacious 2-bedroom apartment. It wasn't unusual to see Moon darting along against the wall, with Bandito lunging at her from underneath the furniture, and Tedward on the inside track, adopting a kangaroo-like posture in order to grab Bandito with his front paws and drag him out.

It's true that Moon was an unusual rat. At some point she discovered how much fun it was to annoy my goldfish, Spirit. Spirit lived in a large, wide-mouthed fish bowl on the kitchen counter. Moon taught herself to jump up and grab the hanging dishtowel and swing herself up like a little monkey and get up on the countertop. One day I came into the kitchen and saw Moon perched on the rim of the bowl, cupping her front paws in the water and drinking. Then I noticed Spirit seemed to be moving at a brisk pace around the perimeter of the bowl, even coming out of the water a bit at times. Suddenly Moon froze, eyeing the circling fish—then jerked her body forward and made a grab for her. At this brazen act, Spirit leaped ahead and started swimming even faster. Moon was swaying on the edge of the bowl, following every movement. I realized this was a game, one that probably had been played before.

One afternoon I was sitting on our couch, eating chocolate ice cream, with Moon perched on my shoulder and gladly accepting the occasional taste. I noticed that she perked her ears when we heard the jingling of Tedward's collar as he trotted down the hallway on his way into the living room. Moon climbed off of me and crossed the cushion to the arm of the couch, and hunkered down right at the edge. When Tedward came swinging around the corner, she launched herself into the air and landed on his back! I watched, amazed, as Tedward began gyrating like a bucking bronco, turning his head to get at her, and Moon hanging on to the guard hairs on his shoulders and riding him as long as she could. She was soon "bucked off", and Tedward quickly turned and pinned her to the floor, growling. She writhed and squealed and was soon let free, only to dash at Tedward's toes and take a nip. It looked like Moon got about 18 inches of air on that leap.

When I told Holly about it, she sounded skeptical. "Pearsonnnnn, you wouldn't be pulling my leg, would you?" I swore it was true, and agreed to set up the same scenario to see if it would happen again. A couple of days later, 2 other friends from the Mammal Center came over, and I got out the ice cream, told Tedward to stay in the kitchen for a minute, and put Moon on my shoulder. The others stayed quiet as I fed Moon a few tiny bites and then called Tedward. Danged if it didn't happen again, exactly the same way! Too bad YouTube wouldn't exist for another quarter century.

Chapter 2

After our California interlude, we once again turned our faces toward our beloved Rocky Mountains, where Tedward had his beginning. But we took an unusual route: we arranged a ride with a college student on his way to Phoenix, who very kindly went way out of his way to drop us off in a field near Tucson. It was around midnight and the air smelled of unusual plants; I could hardly wait until morning to take a look at them. This was my first sojourn as an adult into the Sonoran Desert.

Tedward, now about 2, proved to be a great traveling companion. We walked through town the next morning with our packs on—yes, Tedward had his own dog pack filled with kibble—heading toward Tucson Mountain Park. It rained hard that night and we ended up under my tube tent which I draped over a picnic table. When it began to get light and the rain stopped, we crawled out of our den and surveyed the large expanse of desert surrounded by jagged mountains on 3 sides. The air was cool and fragrant, and there was a surprising amount of greenery. As I was preparing to fry some Jimmy Dean sausage over the campfire, my mini-percolator full of Kona coffee started to bubble. The smell of the coffee mixed with the sharp smell of the sage and other plants was intoxicating. Then the sun rose just underneath the cloud bank, and the rays shot over the landscape, lighting up every drop of rainwater still clinging to the leaves and cactus needles. It was like being surrounded by millions of miniature, quivering diamonds. That was one of the most beautiful moments I ever experienced—and Tedward and I had it all to ourselves.

After spending about a week in the Tucson area, I decided to head east to Las Cruces, New Mexico, to look up an old family friend. Since

the Greyhound didn't allow dogs on board—how is that fair?—I girded my loins and prepared to hitchhike. I ate breakfast in a diner in
Benton, Arizona, chatting with a large Texas truck driver and swilling
several cups of coffee to gain courage, while Tedward waited outside
guarding the packs. Finally I was ready. After munching the bites of
steak and eggs I brought him, Tedward stood patiently while I fastened
the straps of his pack, and we headed to the freeway ramp. As my mind
temporarily stopped it's worrying and focused on the difficulty of getting us over the huge cattle guard at the beginning of the ramp, I heard
a voice yell, "Young lady, young lady!" I looked around and there was
a bushy-headed man waving to me from the gas station on the corner. When he saw me looking he shouted, "Are you going to Texas?"
I answered that no, I was just going as far as Las Cruces, and he said
"C'mon, you kin ride with us!"

Hmmm. Riding with strangers—not something I'm real comfortable with, but at least I'd get a chance to check these people out a bit
first, instead of having to make a split-second decision on the side of
the freeway. Tedward and I made our way over to a truly ancient flatbed
Ford pickup, with the bearded man alongside putting gas in the tank. He
introduced himself as Kenny, and pointed to another decrepit-looking
truck, this one a Chevy, saying that his friend Joseph was driving it with
his 2 great grand-kids and a litter of puppies along for the ride. Kenny
asked if Tedward could ride in back on the flatbed, tied to the cab. I
looked down at my buddy and said, "Well?" and he looked pretty relaxed, so I took that as a yes. Then Joseph and the 2 children, about 7
and 10 years of age, walked over to meet us. Joseph said they were mi-
grant workers, on their way to Texas for the potato harvest. Their hands
and clothes were dirty, but they seemed allright, and the kids were very
friendly, expressing interest in Tedward. Joanie, the older child, took my
hand and led me over to the Chevy and pointed in the passenger-side
window, saying "Look!" On the floor was a friendly-looking mixed breed
dog, with 5 small pups squirming at her belly.

I rode with Kenny in the flatbed, and Tedward, with his ears flapping, appeared to enjoy being out in the wind. The engine noise was so loud we couldn't really converse—also the fact that Kenny had no teeth made understanding him a bit challenging. I did hear him say the truck was a 1946—with almost every part still original. We'd only been on the road about 20 minutes when Joseph, driving ahead of us at 45 miles per hour on Interstate 10, signaled with his arm out the window for the next exit. We followed him as he pulled into a coffee shop. As we piled out, Joseph hollered that it was time for "cup of coffee number two". As the day went on, and our little caravan stopped at every single coffee shop on the side of the freeway, I realized we weren't going to make it to Las Cruces in the normal 4 hours. But what the heck—Tedward and I were on vacation.

I also noticed that Joseph and Kenny stopped every time they saw a vehicle on the side of the freeway, to see if they needed any help. Wow. They would whip out whatever tools they needed and work until they solved the problem, and if it was more than they could manage, they offered to alert the nearest gas station so a tow truck could be sent. And those kids were pretty cool. Joseph told me, over about the 5th cup of coffee, that Joanie had "saved his bacon" the year before, when he had a heart attack while driving. She guided the truck to safety, then called on the CB for help. The boy, Jason, challenged me to a rock-throwing contest outside. Joanie joined in, and I marveled at the fact that these kids, though not growing up in a way most people would consider traditional, were friendly, considerate, and polite.

As the sun was sinking and we were approaching Las Cruces, I wondered how the meeting would go between these decent, though rough and uneducated people, and Roy Harmon, a well-off Native American who'd been successful in his profession of hospital administrator. (We had arranged to meet at a restaurant on the edge of town, as I had called Roy from a pay phone about 2 hours before.) I needn't have worried. Everybody got along like a house on fire. Even Roy's 14-year-old son,

Tedward, a.k.a. "Little Pud", soon after arriving at the Oldhams'.

Tedward not afraid to challenge Nikki to a tug of war

who seemed at first like a typical sulky butthead of a teenager, was soon outside running around with Jason and Joanie, while Roy and Kenny and Joseph were looking under the hood of Kenny's pickup and discussing the finer points of engine maintenance. Roy treated us all to a hearty lunch, and we shook hands and said goodbye. As I was unpacking in the spare room at Roy's house, with Tedward munching his dinner, I did notice one thing—my wallet was missing. I don't remember how much money was in it, but there was one of my favorite pictures of my Dad in there, of him sitting on a DC-10 with a cup of coffee in his hand, with every seat taken by other businessmen in long-sleeved white shirts and narrow ties. He apparently didn't know someone was taking his picture, because he was looking out the airplane window with a sort of bemused expression. Dang, I wish I still had that picture.

The next morning, Roy was telling me about Lake Roberts, in the Gila Wilderness Area, and some nearby Indian ruins. He suggested I take his old van and go up there and check it out. He didn't have to twist my arm. After visiting for a decent interval, I loaded up and took off. Little did I know that in the area that Tedward and I began to explore, there would be a return of wild wolves about 25 years later!

You couldn't park right by the lake shore, so I pulled into the parking lot of a rock shop. A white-haired old man was puttering around outside, and I asked him where we could camp for the night. He looked me up and down, then he looked at Tedward, who was standing relaxed by my side, and said, "aw heck, you can park right there", and he pointed to a corner of the lot under a large tree. He told me I could sleep right on the lakeshore if I wanted, if I didn't mind the old Indian spirits that might be roaming around. Hmmm. I walked with him into the shop and noticed he had a pretty great collection of agates, geodes, fossils and other things. There was also plenty of dust. We got to talking some more, and I told him Tedward and I were on a trip to explore a little of the country before heading back to Colorado. He seemed to think that was reasonable, which was refreshing, because many people find it a bit peculiar—a young woman and a dog, traveling alone.*

After dishing up Tedward's food and preparing some delicious macaroni and cheese on my tiny camp stove, we ate and then walked around the lake as the sun was setting. I remember waking up in the night with a full moon shining on us, and everything covered with frost, including Tedward's rear end and tail, which were the only parts that were showing, as he'd crammed himself into my mummy bag as far as he was able. I realized my forehead and eyelashes were also frosty. We were in a sparkling wonderland, and it was perfectly quiet, with no wind, no insects, and no traffic noise. The silence was so complete, it was almost like it had its own sound, if that makes any sense.

The next morning, we explored some slot canyons around the Mimbres River. There was no one around, and Tedward was able to range freely. I'd never experienced this type of canyon before. The sandy floors were perfectly flat, and the rock walls, which topped out about 50 feet overhead, became more and more narrow as you advanced up a gentle incline. I remember getting to a place in one of them where I could no longer continue. The end of the canyon was only a few feet ahead. There was a drip of water coming from above, and a bowl-shaped depression at eye level where the water must have been hitting for an awfully long time. Tedward was able to squeeze forward and raising up on his hind legs, drank some of the water, as I gazed up at the blue gash of the sky overhead, aware of the cool stone pressing against my bare arms.

Later, we found a deer trail and worked our way up to the top of the mesa, and laid down to rest under the scant shade of a pinyon pine. Once again the silence was surreal, but it was soon broken by the shrill calls of a small flock of pinyon jays, which zoomed so close to us it caused Tedward to jump up and bark. I was glad he had sense enough not to give chase, as we were perched on a narrow butte with canyons dropping down on both sides of us. After sharing some trail mix and water from the canteen, we slithered back down to valley floor and made our way over to the river. I couldn't believe the quantity and variety of colorful stones, on the bank and in the river itself. We spent the rest of the afternoon in and out of the water, and I ended up with several pounds of gorgeous rocks to add to my collection. While exploring, I saw a dead raven lying in a shady spot not far from the water. It seemed perfectly whole, and I stroked its glossy feathers, wondering how it had died. I looked over my shoulder at it as I walked away, and saw the wind lift the edge of one wing.

Although I had heard and seen ravens before, it wasn't until I experienced their presence here in New Mexico that I really began to feel a bond with them as a species. Their deep croaks and melodious calls echoed among the canyons as they flew around on their raven business. And in the silence you could distinctly hear the sound of their wings as they passed overhead. Sharing this beautiful wilderness area with Tedward and the ravens and the river and nature in all its forms, left memories that I cherish to this day.

Chapter 3

When Roy dropped me and Tedward off at the freeway ramp, there was a guy about my age with a backpack nearby. He had a dog that looked a bit liked Tedward. The 3 of us conversed for a bit, then I thanked Roy for a great 2 weeks in New Mexico, and we said goodbye. The young guy, Rick, asked if I would consider hitchhiking together, as it was easier for a couple to get a ride than one guy alone. He seemed like a decent sort, so I agreed.

About 10 minutes later, a luxurious-looking van pulled up with 2 young ladies in the front. They saw our dogs and apologized, saying they couldn't take us because one of the girls was allergic. Oh man, it looked like the perfect ride. Rick had spent the night by the freeway, so he was especially disappointed. We ended up waiting several hours before a Mexican guy with a big pickup stopped and said he could take us as far as Albuquerque. We put the dogs and our packs in the back, climbed aboard, and soon I was saying my prayers as the driver goosed it up to 85. Then he pulled out a joint, and shows it to us with a question in his eyes. Rick looked at me and I raised my eyebrows, which he took as a yes, so we proceeded to get ourselves into a state where those buttes with the afternoon light hitting them were really, really pretty.

When we were dropped off near the university in Albuquerque, I made the decision to leave some of my rocks on an outside table for someone else to take and enjoy; I just couldn't take lugging around that extra weight. (If I only knew I'd be carrying twice my own body weight in the future, oy). I forget where we spent the night, but there was no hanky-panky; Rick was a gentleman, and I was not in the habit of... well, you know. We parted ways in Boulder, Colorado, and after taking only 2 rides to get all that way, it took Tedward and I 4 rides just to get from Boulder to Estes Park!

By now it was April (1978), and Tedward and I freeloaded off various friends until getting hired at Grouse Creek Livery, 5 miles west of Vail. Our old buddy Chris landed a summer job at Piney Lake, another horseback outfit, not far from there. Grouse Creek was on Forest Service land, which was great because Tedward could come along on the rides—that is, until our boss, Dave, banned him. In fact, Tedward got banned several times over the course of the next 2 summers, but Dave would eventually forget or relent, and Tedward would be free once again to find new and creative ways to drive "Bossman" to distraction.

The first memorable incident was in early June, when I had 2 ladies from Denver on a breakfast ride. I was on my horse Joe, and the guests were on Lightning and Thundercloud, 2 mares who were very calm, which turned out to be very lucky. We were winding up through the aspens with the morning sun shining through the leaves, on our way to a "cowboy breakfast". Suddenly there came a god-awful roaring, snarling, and thrashing sound from down the slope. The ladies, alarmed, asked what it was, and I told them I wasn't sure, but it might have something to do with my dog Tedward. The hubbub subsided and we continued on, but both humans and horses were on the alert. We didn't have long to wait; the second Joe stepped foot into a small clearing, the outrageous din was right ahead of us. Out of a thick stand of lodgepole pines burst Tedward, running for all he was worth—with 2 coyotes right on his tail. There was instant and total bedlam as I spurred Joe and galloped toward them, shouting. In a heartbeat it was over, Tedward standing almost under Joe's belly, panting heavily, the ladies with their eyes wide and mouths open, but still in the saddle, and the coyotes nowhere in sight. I caught Tedward's grateful glance and said, "Thanks for not bringing back a bear."

The upshot of this incident was, these coyotes apparently decided it would behoove them not to kill this dog, but rather to accord him a certain measure of respect, due to the fact he had what appeared to be a rather large and dangerous protector. But they made one last try: A few days later, a lone coyote showed up on the hillside above our saddling barn, sat on his haunches and broke into song. He kept it up for quite some time, and the other wranglers and I puzzled about this unusual behavior. But where was Tedward? After thinking about it, I decided this coyote was "calling" him to come out and play. I finally found him, skulking around in the tackroom with a hunted look on his face. He refused to come out. The coyote finally gave up and melted back into the trees. A short time later, one of our wranglers, a tall, lanky kid from Tennessee named Jeff, tapped me on the shoulder and said, "Check that out", while pointing to the south. There strolled 2 coyotes, making their way up the hill. My guess is, Tedward had a feeling the songster had a partner, and that those were probably the same two dog-chasing varmints he'd encountered a few days before.

The next installment of the "coyote show" happened later that week. I had 14 people behind me on an afternoon ride, traversing a large open slope. The fragrant summer breeze was waving the grasses and wildflowers, the sun was shining, and all was peaceful and lovely. Then somebody in the back yelled, "Look at that!" We all swiveled our heads and caught sight of Tedward, loping along a track parallel to ours, with a single coyote following him. Their tongues were lolling, and there was a certain rocking-horse look to their gait, which led me to believe that this wasn't a life-or-death sort of chase. All my riders started talking at once, and the horses were turning their heads and pricking their ears at the rarely-seen spectacle of a wild and domestic canine interacting. One after the other, Tedward and the coyote galloped into a stand of trees, and were lost to our view. The tension was palpable as we held our course, waiting—and suddenly the coyote appeared, loping out of the shadows, running back the way he'd come—with Tedward chasing him! This totally delighted my guests, many of whom were surprised that there was no animosity being displayed, and that not only had Tedward emerged unscathed, but he'd "turned the tables on the wily coyote", as one man put it. Another gentleman closer to the front loudly proclaimed, "Wow, that ol' hound dog of yours must have some mighty big cojones!" I didn't have to heart to tell him they'd been removed, quite some time ago.

Of all the livery stables I worked at, Grouse Creek was the only one that had a night pasture so big that we had to use our own horses to round up the others in the morning. I had the bright idea that we could teach Tedward to help us, thereby allowing us a few minutes more sleep in the mornings. Also I was always looking for ways to endear Tedward to our boss. He was currently on Dave's "shit list" because he chose to eat a marmot right in front of the pre-schoolers' fence next to the ski lodge where we were bunked. I'm not sure if he actually dispatched the marmot himself, or if he just found it. I was sitting in the reservation kiosk when Dave's Tony Lamas clunked on the wood floor, he jerked his pipe out of his mouth and said in his terse monotone, "Get your dog, he's grossing out the kids", with a jerk of his head towards the lodge. As I approached I saw several wide-eyed toddlers plastered to the fence, staring as Tedward happily munched on a large marmot that was lying on his back with what looked like a little smile on his face. Either he died happy or he was pleased with Tedward's table manners, because the hind third of the marmot was missing, but there was no gory mess. I lugged the surprisingly heavy carcass up the hill, Tedward objecting all the way. I told him if he had to eat something that once was alive, maybe he could be a little more discreet about it.

Anyway, back to the roundup. Things didn't work out quite as I'd planned. Tedward became so engrossed in chasing the running horses that he would not listen to reason. He was soon out of my sight, so I gathered up a small group of 2 of our mares and their gelding buddies, and started on my way back to the barn. After about a minute I heard Tedward in full cry ahead of me, hidden by a small ridge. As I topped it with my bunch, I saw a large dustcloud and in the midst of it was our hero, hauling ass after our old friends Lightning and Thundercloud. This would have been okay, though it was preferable to have them going at something slower than a dead run—but the thing was, he was chasing them toward the west, and the barn was to the north.

I quickly scanned the area to make sure no one was watching, and proceeded to bellow at Tedward to come. He was so caught up in the pursuit that it was as if I didn't exist. I wasn't going to chase after them and lose my group, so I continued on, hoping for the best. As the other wranglers came in with horses, they asked where Tedward was, and did he find any horses to herd. I said oh yes, he found some allright; he should be here any minute. It was 45 minutes later that Lightning and Thundercloud jogged down to the barn, alone, and lathered up like they'd just run the Kentucky Derby. Oh man. Luckily Dave was not around. Tedward must have known he was in deeper doodoo than ever, because he did not show his face until about 2 hours later, when he was suddenly next to me on one of my rides. He had a guilty grin on his face, as I looked at him with reproach. "Well, so much for your horse-herding career", I said. I could imagine his reply: "Yeah, but man, that was a righteous blast".

Naturally Tedward was permanently banned from the roundup. I pretty much gave up going also, mainly to make sure he didn't try to surprise us and join in. But he still found plenty of ways to entertain himself. It didn't take him long to discover that Dan, our cook, sometimes left entire huge trays of raw steaks unattended in the kitchen, while he was in the process of loading up the truck in preparation for our twice-weekly chuckwagon supper rides. I was coming down the hallway toward the kitchen one day when I saw Tedward standing up ahead near the entryway. There was something odd about his posture, like he was slightly sunk down on his legs, and he was peering around the corner, as if he didn't want to be seen. I stopped in my tracks and waited to see what he was up to. I could hear banging and scraping through the open front door, which I knew had to be Dan at the pickup. Tedward quickly trotted across the open area and into the kitchen, made a right turn—and just when I got to where I could see him—lifted one front paw to the counter and took a massive rib-eye in his teeth and eased it off the tray on the counter, whirling and taking off for the open side door in one smooth motion. I didn't stop him and followed him outside, waiting out of sight on the deck to hear Dan's reaction. I wasn't disappointed. A second after I heard his boots in the kitchen, there was a booming "Goddamnit!" that resounded through the lodge. I chuckled as I headed for the barn, marveling at Tedward's stealth and chutzpah.

The only live thing I ever saw him catch was a blue grouse. I was riding Joe alone through a lush grassy area among some aspens, with Tedward scouting ahead. Suddenly a small covey flew up ahead of him at a steep angle, wings whirring. Darned if he didn't leap up and knock one down with a paw! He lowered his head into the grass, and must have killed it right then, because the next instant he was strutting around, showing off his limp prize. I wasn't particularly thrilled that he killed it, but part of me was glad to know he could catch his own food if he had to. As Joe and I moved out into the open, I looked back and saw Tedward drop the grouse and shake his head, as if trying to get the feathers out of his mouth. Perhaps he was thinking that he preferred mammal meat.

In August came Tedward's crowning achievement of the summer. Mike, Chris, Jeff and I had just finished helping our guests dismount at the chuckwagon site, after leading them up the steep, winding trail. This was a beautiful spot, a gently sloping meadow surrounded by as-pens and lodgepoles, with a striking view of the jagged mountains to the west, and not a sign of man to be seen. As we were tying the last of the horses to the thick ropes we had strung between the aspen trunks, we became aware of raucous laughter coming from below. This was a group of men in their 60's, Elk's Club, I believe. We looked over to the cook site, where the guys were standing around with their mulled wine, and Dan laboring over the steaks on the fire. Several of the guests were looking down and to their left—and then we saw Tedward prance into view carrying a large, dried, flattened marmot, definitely dead—and so big it was sticking way out of his mouth on both sides and in the front. This ludicrous sight was generating alot of amusement, and adding to it was one man who shouted, "Guess we're havin' marmot stew!" I covered my mouth, horror and laughter mingling, as Chris said to me, "Better get to him before Dave does." and I hurried down the hill.

Tedward saw me coming and tried to evade my lunge for his collar by insinuating himself into the crowd, causing even more hilarity, as the guests tried to avoid having the dessicated marmot brush against their legs. I managed to get Tedward out of the dining area and make him drop the marmot without having to touch it myself. I pointed sternly in the direction of the barn and said, "Go home!" He started down the back trail, with only one pause and wistful look over his shoulder. His shoulders slumped a little as he trotted off, and I felt guilty for spoiling his fun. As I walked back through the cooking area, I was told by several people that Tedward should be allowed to stay, and that this was the most fun they'd had at an event in years. I smiled sheepishly and admitted that he was often entertaining, but that my boss found him infuriating, to which they guffawed, one man saying, "You just send your bossman over to us, little lady—we'll set 'im straight!"

As I made my way back to the horses, I noticed Chris and the others were wearing huge grins. They asked if I'd seen Dave; I said, "No, thank God". But someone let the cat out of the bag, because the next morning, there were the Tony Lamas in the booth again, and the gravelly voice saying, "No more dog on the chuckwagon supper rides!"

Before the next one, I tied Tedward up to the porch rail, ignoring the beams of annoyance and disbelief emanating from his eyes. The minute we were mounted and headed up the trail, he began howling like a banshee. We could hear it for a good 20 minutes. One rider commented on his "good set of lungs". Thankfully Dave was already up at the cooksite, out of earshot. The ride after that, I told Tedward to stay quiet and not follow us, and I'd leave him free, and that his job was to guard the lodge and not let anyone inside.

The whole way up to the cooksite, I was paranoid. Every time Joe flicked his ears or looked at anything, I thought, this is it, it's Tedward, and we're busted. Even if I could order him back home, at least one of the 14 riders behind me would see him, and the news would get out. But he didn't show himself on the trail. I tried to relax, but the whole evening my glance was darting around the perimeter, almost certain that if he did decide to come up there, he would be sneaky about it, knowing that he was currently in the doghouse, and he wouldn't come all the way out into the open. But there was no sign of him.

As usual it was almost dark by the time we got everybody back to the barn. After helping the guests off their horses and wishing them goodnight, and putting the horses to bed, I rushed back to the lodge to see what Tedward was doing. There he was, lying serenely on the deck, front paws crossed and dangling over the highest step. He gazed at me in a rather cool manner, I thought, as I praised him for doing what I asked. He wasn't above scarfing down the leftover steak I'd brought him though.

A couple of days later, a friend of Chris's came up the barn, and told us he'd tried to return a book Chris had loaned him, "...but a brown dog wouldn't let me up the steps." Chris and I looked at each other. Tedward, who was just passing by on his way to the ground squirrel area to do some chasing, stopped as I hailed him. "Good boy—so you really did guard the lodge!" I swear he looked offended, as if he thought I doubted his ability to understand English. I knew it was also possible that at some point during the evening my crafty canine had snuck up the hill to spy on us at dinner, and made sure to beat us back down the trail so he could assume his innocent pose on the deck. I wonder how many of the Elk's Club guys still remember his shenanigans that night, those that are still alive, that is. Wish I'd realized at the time that those 2 summers at Grouse Creek Livery would be some of the most fun and interesting in my life. I guess I thought every year would be that exciting, because I didn't even bother to take any pictures!*

Nikki and Chuck

Nikki about to ask Joe for the "porch password"

Chapter 4

Tedward had one more little coyote adventure at the end of that summer, when we closed operations at Grouse Creek, but still had a couple of weeks to go at the Keystone stable. I have only a vague memory of the trails there, but I vividly remember one horseback ride that Chris and I took on our half-day off, accompanied of course by Tedward. Chris was mounted on his bay gelding Badger, and I was on Joe as we came to the top of a rise that overlooked a large sage flat, with ponderosa pines encroaching to the north. Tedward, who'd taken off ahead of us and been out of our sight for awhile, appeared down below us, running hard in pursuit of a coyote. Here we go again, I thought, as Chris and I watched. But something was off, because the coyote didn't seem to be running at full speed, like Tedward was. In fact, judging by the way she would glance back now and then, it looked like he—or she—was kind of hoping Tedward would catch up. Now it is known that female coyotes in heat will lure dogs on a merry chase, sometimes ending in something a lot more dramatic and dangerous than an interspecies frolic. Sure enough, as I moved my gaze farther along in the direction they were running, I spotted 2 coyotes, hidden in the pines, keenly watching the chase. Chris saw them at the same time I did, and he was right behind me as Joe and I thundered down the slope with me in full cry. Tedward was completely focused on the chase—no surprise there—and it wasn't until I was almost on top of him that he finally pulled up and came out of his trance. I noticed the coyote looked back once more, with what I fancied was a disappointed expression on her face. "Tedward, just because you've made friends with the Grouse Creek coyotes, doesn't mean the Keystone pack or any others are going to want to be associated with you in a friendly way", I scolded, as he stood there panting heavily, looking at me with mingled relief and annoyance. I figured that was the second time I'd saved his bacon. I was amused at myself for automatically glancing around to make sure no one except Chris had seen. The image of Dave's disapproving scowl was forever imprinted on my brain, even though Dave himself was several miles away at Grouse Creek.

After the Keystone interlude was over, Chris worked at Piney Lake awhile longer, and he let me borrow Sam, his red jeep pickup, to take a little camping trip with Tedward. We found a nice place by a picnic area to spend the night, and we were the only ones there. It was October, and many of the aspens still had their beautiful yellow leaves. I laid out my down bag not far from Sam, and Tedward crossed the nearby creek and explored the meadow on the other side, while I got dinner ready. After gorging ourselves on beef stew, with the usual Kibbles and Bits for my buddy, we settled down for the night, the campfire gently crackling. Ahhh, so quiet, so peaceful. How did I know it wouldn't last? Some time later, as I turned in my bag so I faced the creek, I glimpsed a stealthy-looking 4-legged form, smaller than a breadbox, silhouetted against the moonlight on the water. Tedward was sound asleep on my opposite side. I waited, knowing it was only a matter of time before whatever it was betrayed its presence to Tedward. I must have fallen asleep, because it came as a surprise when he growled and stiffened next to me, and I knew he was getting ready to take off. I struggled to get my arms out of my bag to grab him, but I was too late. The moon had set, making everything pitch black, and when I finally freed my arms and sat up with my legs still in the bag, I couldn't see a thing, but I could hear Tedward dashing away from me. Then I heard an odd little whine, and what I thought might be his paws skidding to a halt. Then came the sound of the running feet again, but this time they were coming back toward me. Suddenly Tedward leaped out of the gloom, diving and rolling on my down bag—and a second later the smell hit me. It was like a smoky, rolling cloud—our first close encounter with a skunk!

Too bad he had to include me in this little drama. I tried to push him off, but he avoided my shoves, ignored my yells and curses, and kept trying to wipe the smell off on me and my heretofore sweet-smelling bag. There was no escaping from the powerful odor, as I'm sure you can imagine. It was a bit different than the sharp stench of a skunk hit on the road. It was somehow deeper, and at that range, all-encompassing. It was as if all the pores of my body were inhaling it.

I mulled over the possibilities. Try washing him in the creek? No, not on a chilly night. Put him in Chris's truck? Definitely not. I finally decided to tie him, and secured him with a rope to the handle of the truck—several yards from me. I guess I could have slept inside Sam, but with our luck I'd wake up to Tedward trying to mix it up with a bear or mountain lion while still tied. I held my breath and climbed back into my bag. I tied a bandanna over my nose and mouth, and somehow was able to sleep. We drove back down the mountain with the bag and Tedward in the back, airing out. When I stepped out in front of Chris's cabin at Piney Lake, he opened the door, caught a whiff, and immediately knew what had happened. Did he get mad? No—he didn't even act surprised. In 2 hours, we were smelling alot better—me, Sam, Tedward, and even my bag, which we sprayed with an assortment of air fresheners, deodorizers, and even some Old Spice. That bag never quite regained it's sweet smell, but it as Chris said, it had alot more character now.

Chris got Tedward to take another bath the next day, by throwing "sticks" in the Eagle River for him. I was looking on the bank for a few of suitable size, and when I turned around, there was Chris heaving a huge log into the water! Tedward gamely ran into the river and started swimming for it. I thought, no way can he bring that thing back, especially with the current and all. At first he tried grabbing it in the middle, but realized he couldn't make any headway, so he shifted his grip to one end, and allowing his head to turn, pulled the log back to shore.

From then on, during several more fetches, he went to the nearest end and hauled it in. Chris stopped after about 7 throws, though Tedward looked as if he wanted the game to continue. My neck got sore just watching him.

That night, Tedward and I slept in the large meadow below Piney Lake. I borrowed a sleeping bag, as mine was still convalescing. Chris and I had stuffed ourselves senseless earlier at one of our favorite eating establishments, the Saddle Rock Supper Club, near Leadville. My hair was really short then, and when we walked in, I had turned to the side to say something to Chris, and we heard the hostess say, "Be with you fellas in a minute." I have rarely heard Chris laugh the way he did then. There was a donkey-like quality to it. And he never forgot that little scene—to this day, if my hair is short, he has to bring that up. (Just like he brings up the fact that I weigh twice as much now as I did then.)

Anyway, as Tedward and I settled down for the night, we could hear coyotes sounding off in the trees a distance behind us. I admonished Tedward not to get any ideas, saying, "Remember what almost happened to you at Keystone", among other things. But of course he couldn't resist. I woke up later to the amazing clear and moonless starstrewn sky, then realized my buddy was not curled up next to me—in fact, he was nowhere to be seen. I sighed, laid back on my pillow, listened, and waited. I didn't hear any dog or coyote vocalizations, but in a few minutes I caught the sound of the muted thump of his paws on the grass as he galloped back to me. He was panting and seemed a little nervous. I could see him in the starlight, but not too well. I felt him all over, and found a wet spot on one foreleg. I turned the flashlight on it, and it was bloody, but not too bad; a typical bite wound. I got out my little first aid kit, and cleaned and dressed it. He looked a little chagrined, as I reminded him of what I'd told him earlier. "Many things you learn so quickly, like how to efficiently pull a large log from the river. But you can't seem to get it that the Grouse Creek coyotes are your only coyote 'friends'!"

Chapter 5

Thinking of all the running going on lately—dog, coyote, and horse—reminded me of a certain horse race that took place 2 years before, in the summer of 1974. Chris and I were working for Moraine Park Stables, in Rocky Mountain National Park—it was the first trail guiding job for both of us. We had horses, but no dogs then, as this was "B.T."—Before Tedward. I believe Chris was mounted on his favorite gelding Buck that day, and Jeff our wrangler from Indiana, (not to be confused with Tennessee Jeff of Grouse Creek) was riding a somewhat hyper sorrel named Skip, who he was constantly touting as the "fastest horse in the stable." Jeff had 4 people on the 2-o'clock ride to Cub Lake. Neither Chris nor I had a 4-o'clock ride, so when we finished tidying up the barn and the saddling chute, we decided to take our horses out and meet Jeff and his riders on their way back. I hopped on Joe bareback, and Chris shuddered. "There's a reason saddles were invented", he intoned in his deep bass voice, as I chuckled. I told him it may still be a man's world, but there were some advantages to being female.

We rode off briskly, breaking the park rules ("horses are to be kept to a walk on the trails") several times, and managed to avoid running over any hikers as we loped over the aspen-lined curves of the flat part of the trail. We saw Jeff just coming down off the first steep section with his guests—a congenial couple with 2 kids, aged about 12 and 15. We sat on our horses and shot the breeze for a few minutes, then Jeff and company continued back toward the barn, and Chris and I took our horses upwards for a ways. We soon turned back, and caught up with Jeff on the gravel road that was pretty close to the barn. We decided to pass Jeff at a lope, knowing that would aggravate him, since he couldn't go fast with riders behind. I gave him a smirk as Joe and I breezed by, and Jeff had to hold Skip tight, as he was having a hissy fit at our coming up on him like that. Jeff met my eyes, hesitated for a second while Skip pitched and yawed under him, and then suddenly dropped his hand down to Skip's neck. That old nag took off like a rocket, with Joe doing the same, both horses scrabbling on the gravel for purchase as they quickly gained their stride and thundered down the road neck and neck. I was scared but exhilarated, making a half-hearted attempt to rein Joe in, but there was absolutely no way he was going to miss his chance to race another horse. I managed to glance back without falling off—no saddle, remember—and glimpsed the amusing sight of Chris right behind us on Buck, who was galloping gamely, with Chris holding up his arm across his eyes to avoid being pinged by the gravel that Skip was kicking up. And the riders? All four were hauling ass behind—sticking to their saddles like glue. I'm pretty sure it was the dad I heard yelling, "Hyah, hyah!" Tears were literally whipped from my eyes as I prayed the road, which was accessible to cars along there, would stay clear. We leaned around the last bend, the horses pelting toward the open gate, with Joe edging in front right at the last. We had to pull up hard to avoid a totally blind curve and make the turn toward the barn. I was exulting over my victory, and it was aw-fully hard to keep it to myself. It was especially sweet because Joe didn't look fast, and he wasn't young—he was 16! And it would hopefully put a stopper on Jeff's insufferable bragging about that nag of his. We checked on our followers, and all were intact. I couldn't believe Jeff did that—putting his riders at risk and all. Chris and I speculated later that possibly all flatland Indiana cowboys might be equally insane.

Jeff was muttering at the dinner table and during our nightly card game that the race wasn't fair because Joe didn't have a saddle, which added alot of weight. Oh, and let's not forget that Skip was much more tired than Joe, having just come off the trail. After enduring the slights and thinly-veiled insults about my personal integrity and the ability of my horse to win a "real" contest, I finally threw down my cards and challenged him to a rematch, with both of us riding bareback, and Ella and Danny, our 2 junior wranglers, posted at the beginning and end of the route as witnesses to make sure the race was run fairly. Of course I knew there was no way in hell Jeff would agree to race without saddles; I just wanted to drive home the fact that just maybe I could do something on a horse that he couldn't. So it was set, saddles to be used, at 7 a.m. the next day. A morning race would ensure both horses were fresh.

Ella chose to stand at the "finish line", which was good because I knew she'd be rooting for me and Joe, and would overlook any shenanigans we might pull to gain an edge. I did briefly contemplate putting a piece of crinkly plastic in my pocket, and throwing it Skip's way if he seemed to be gaining; he was spooky about that kind of stuff. And I knew Jeff wouldn't be above that sort of thing himself. But I decided to trust that Joe and I could beat those varmints. I forget what was the starting signal—but I know it wasn't a pistol, since no firearms were allowed in the national park. After getting the all clear from Ella, Danny said ready, set, go or whatever it was, and we were off. It was a similar thrill-ride, only with a saddle you can't feel the incredible power of the horse's body beneath you to the same degree. I once again marveled at Joe's apparent singlemindedness; I'd never raced him before, and never thought he'd be so into it. Lo and behold—we won, but not by much. Ella raised her arms and yelled, "Joe by a head!" and danced around. I tried to not be too overtly ecstatic, but it wasn't easy, as everybody now had hard evidence that my horse—my old, big-bellied, short-legged Quarter Horse Joe—was faster than the slim, flashy-looking Skip.

Jeff did not speak to me for 2 days. I think Chris was secretly glad I'd won, but he couldn't show it at the risk of harming male solidarity. Jeff and I did become something of an item that summer, but it took a little while for him to recover from the drubbing Joe and I gave him. I had an interesting conversation with Joe's former owner, and not only was Joe a former cow horse, but he was also used to pony race horses out to the starting gate at Bay Meadows in California, and the kids would often race their horses after the official races were done with for the day. That solved the mystery of his competitive zeal. Truly, a horse of many talents.

Chapter 6

In the fall of 1978, I worked as a waitress at the Redstone Inn, in the beautiful Crystal Valley, one big ridge over from Aspen. I remember I got pasture for Joe just down the road for $10 a month, and that included hay when it snowed; a pretty good deal even for those days. I rented a room in the fire chief's house, and Tedward made friends with a small dog named Becky* that belonged to another gal that worked at the inn. Not too much excitement that winter, except for one night. I was off work earlier than Mimi, who liked to whoop it up at the bar after hours. Tedward and Becky were huddled next to me on my bunk, the heater was working overtime, and it was snowing heavily outside. Around 3 a.m. there came the kind of sound guaranteed to startle human and dogs instantly awake: a man roaring and yelling and pounding on our front door. Tedward sucked in a big breath to sound the alarm, but I held his muzzle and whispered "Quiet!" I got out of bed and both dogs jumped down after me, following as I went to John Henry's hall closet and got out his 30-06. I had no clue how to operate it, but I figured just the sight of it might deter someone from mischief.

It was interesting that I never had to tell either dog to be quiet again, especially Becky, who was a notorious yapper. Both of them were at my heels as I carried the gun into the living room, where the noise was even louder, the man shouting to be let in, that he was freezing to death. My heart was hammering as I yelled, "Who is it?", in what I hoped was a confident, alpha-female sort of voice. The man then started on a long, drunken-sounding rant, and I thought I heard him say my housemate's name in there somewhere. Ahhh, I thought, another poor devil she's led on, hoping to stake his claim. I was debating whether to let him in—it really was freezing outside, and even if he had a vehicle, it seemed obvious he was in no shape to drive. I looked at the dogs, who looked back at me like 2 eager midshipmen, waiting for their captain's orders. I unlocked the door, holding the firearm vertical and somewhat behind my back. The guy staggered in, promptly tripped over the nearby footstool, and crashed to the floor. He groaned, turned over, and didn't even attempt to get up. He looked pathetic. I hoped he wasn't going to barf on John Henry's bearskin rug.

I said, "Who are you and what are you doing out in this storm?" He managed to convey that he was a friend of Mimi's and wanted to see her. Yeah, I'll bet, I thought to myself. I said, "Mimi's not here, she's probably at the bar; that's like her second home." I figured he was so drunk he wouldn't remember that last part. Then he shivered, and let out another groan. "Look, why don't you just stay there for awhile and warm up, and maybe she'll be home soon." He meekly agreed, so I told the dogs to stay there and watch him, and I got a blanket, threw it on him, built up the fire, moved the 30-06 to the other side of the room and sat in the easy chair, the dogs laying down close by. It wasn't long before lover-boy was snoring like a hog. I fetched some waxed paper from the kitchen and placed generous pieces of it all around his head.

Some time later, Mimi walked in, took one look around, and said, "Good God, what happened in here?!" I said, "Your 'friend' happened. Now you can take over. I'm going back to bed." I stalked off, and her own dog, after greeting her, followed me into the bedroom. As both dogs jumped onto my bed, Mimi was stridently raising her voice, commanding Becky to come to her. I chuckled to myself. I thought, what a couple of good dogs. And the pint-sized varmint is cool in a crisis, obeys orders, and has good taste to boot.

One other little Mimi story. About 2 years later, she invited me to a Christmas dinner at her condo in Snowmass. She had acquired a second dog, an English Setter mix—I forget his name. She asked me if Tedward could be trusted not to "make a mess" in the house, as she had white carpeting. Somewhat offended, I declared that Tedward was "100% housetrained."

Three guesses as to what happened. 1. It was a pleasant, uneventful night. Wrong. 2. Tedward stole the Christmas ham, and shared it with the other dogs. Wrong again. 3. Tedward turned out to be only 99% housetrained. Bingo. I was sitting on the couch (it was also white; I myself always preferred brown tones for carpeting and furniture, like a normal animal owner) with my head turned, talking to another guest. When I looked back toward the beautiful Christmas tree, there was Tedward, taking a dump right in front of it. Turns out, Mimi's new dog was not even 50% housebroken, and had been regularly violating the pristine snowy carpet in more than one place. Tedward, smelling the evidence of this, must have thought, "Well, when in Rome…".

Chapter 7

It was January of 1979, and I could feel Hawaii calling me. I made arrangements for Joe to be boarded at a ranch in Lyons, owned by Chris's good friend Bob. Tedward was to stay with my buddy Beth, in Leadville. Starting with a large, congenial young man named Henry, who picked me up hitchhiking on my way down to Kealakekua Bay, I ended up meeting an entire extended Hawaiian family, and grew very fond of them. I spent 4 months in Hawaii, then another 3 weeks in California with Holly, Bandito's owner, who now ran the lighthouse at Pillar Point. By the time I got back to Colorado in May, I was suffering from an acute case of critter withdrawal.

Beth and her boyfriend had recently moved to an ancient little cabin on a hillside near Leadville. I could see Beth and Tedward from a distance, as we approached each other on the trail. It was pretty high elevation there, and absolutely gorgeous, with snow still on the peaks and in some of the valleys between. The rest was an incredible shade of emerald green, with a sprinkling of wildflowers here and there. Tedward may have gotten my scent, or recognized my walk, because he got ahead of Beth and was coming fast, ears perked. When he reached me, he raised up and placed one paw on my sternum, gazing earnestly into my eyes, as if to ask, "Is it really you?" I hugged and kissed him and patted him all over, and he became my "shadow", as Beth termed it, from then on.

I thanked Beth for keeping him safe, and as we walked toward the cabin, I asked her how he had behaved. She said he was great, no trouble at all, and was always "part of the circle", when they had friends over. That didn't surprise me. I thought privately that he probably inhaled his share of marijuana smoke too. Beth also told me that he would routinely jump the fence in the yard, and be gone for a couple of hours in the evening, but that he always came back by around 10:00 p.m. I asked if he was cruising around downtown Leadville, and Beth said no, she would have heard about it. (So he wasn't like Rocky, the Irish Setter mix we boarded for awhile in Estes Park, who used to make the rounds of all the restaurants in town every evening) I said, Where do you think he went?" Her guess was, he was roaming the forest which started not far from their house, since they lived on the eastern edge of town. I thought about it, and figured that sounded about right. Either that, or he'd made some other human friends that he visited. I marveled at his independence and intelligence. He could make his own choices, and things usually turned out allright. Well, maybe not according to Dave, whom he would soon get the chance to torment anew, as we were hired to guide trail rides a second summer at Grouse Creek.

His first heinous act that summer of 1979 was to forcefully ram his snout up the backside of a potential customer. He had an unfortunate predilection for this particular behavior. Dave used to refer to this and other tendencies of his as "that dog's nasty little habits." (I figured parading dried marmots in front of guests, eating fresh marmots in front of children, stealing steaks off the kitchen counter and chasing horses the wrong way on the roundup probably all fell into this category). His first victim that year was our female wrangler from Colorado Springs, Claire. After that first violation, Claire started referring to him as "the gooser". One fine morning a few days later I was gazing out the door of the reservation booth at a Rufous hummingbird that was at the feeder, when a pleasant-looking youngish woman wearing a tennis outfit—the kind with the little skirt—walked up to the booth's window. As I swiveled on my stool to greet her I saw Chris and Mike just taking a seat on the bench that ran along side of the barn. The booth was up a step from ground level, so from my perch inside, I could only see people that were standing at the window from about the solar plexus up. As I was giving the woman information about our trail rides, she suddenly said "Oh!" and jumped, then swatted at something behind her, saying, "Get away!" in a very pissed-off voice. In my peripheral vision I saw Mike and Chris writhing as if in pain, and then I spotted Tedward behind the lady, backing up, with the old gleam in his eye.

I struggled mightily to contain the great shout of laughter I could feel rising within me. I was not successful. I wanted to apologize, but I could only bow my head to the countertop while issuing forth a series of odd, wheezing grunts. After a few seconds I was able to gasp out the query, "Where's Dave?" before the laughter overtook me again. I remember dimly hearing Chris's answer: "at the lodge", for which I thanked my lucky stars. When I regained a measure of control and was able to sit up, I saw a cherry-red convertible roaring out of the parking lot.

I'm afraid we lost that customer.

3 of Chris's riders, Moraine Park'

Caryl and Joe; I was trying to imitate Lee Marvin in Cat Ballou,
but I couldn't get Joe to lean like the mule in the movie.

Chapter 8

We had another new wrangler that summer, a big, husky farm girl from Iowa named Sandy. She had sort of a gruff but good-natured way about her. She used to like to get my goat by calling Tedward an "old soup hound" and saying how worthless he was. One day she said, "Too bad that dog of yours would never protect you if you were attacked." I immediately rose to the bait. "How do you know?", I said, irritated. "Maybe we should try a little experiment. You pretend to assault me, and we'll see what he does." I called Tedward over and Sandy grabbed my arm and began punching me—not too lightly either. Tedward watched intently for about 2 seconds, then stepped up to Sandy and grabbed hold of her leg just above the knee. She scoffed and kept up her pummeling, while I said things like, "Ow, stop, you're hurting me!"—which wasn't far from the truth. (Did I mention she was a big girl?) Tedward rolled his eyes so he could watch what was happening, and growling low in his throat, gradually increased the pressure of his teeth on her thigh. At a certain point it was Sandy that said "Ow" and let go of me, and Tedward promptly eased his grip and wisely, I thought, backed away. He was wearing an interesting expression, kind of a knowing leer. Sandy scowled and put her hands on her hips, looked at Tedward and said, "Huh! By golly, maybe he would protect you. I'll be danged." I was proud of him and praised him lavishly. Miss Large-and-in-Charge was proven wrong, and actually had the grace to admit it.

The beauty of it was his sense of judgment. He knew her, but he didn't approve of her actions, so he chose an appropriate way of using force to get her to back off. Sandy gained a new insight into his intelligence from that incident. I don't believe I heard the term "soup hound" again that summer.

I'm going to jump ahead in time to 2 other instances where Tedward perceived possible danger to me and intervened accordingly. One time at Whisman Park in Mountain View, California, I was bird-watching, Tedward was exploring, and we ended up on opposite sides of a large green field. A male jogger was approaching me from my right, as I stood facing Tedward who was nosing around the far edge of the field, where it dropped down into the creek. He lifted his head to check my position, then noticed the jogger. He stared at him briefly, then back at me, then at the jogger again, and then he took off, running toward me. I watched as he changed his angle so that he ended up slightly ahead of me, but on the side the runner was approaching. He wheeled around at the exact point that someone with ill intent would probably choose to veer in my direction. I admired his strategic instincts. Tedward never growled or postured as the man drew nearer, but as he stood there panting from his dash across the field, I knew he was watching him and was ready to protect me if the need arose. As soon as the runner passed, Tedward relaxed and came over to me, and I told him what a good boy he was, and how much I appreciated his vigilance.

The other time was when I was wrestling with my friend Scott on the living room floor of my house in Cupertino. This must have been in 1982. Scott used to be an all-state wrestling champ in high school, and of course he pinned me easily. We were joking about how it was hardly a fair contest, when Tedward suddenly appeared out of nowhere, and went right for the side of Scott's face. He didn't bite, but he gave him a good bump with his teeth. No broken skin, just a little dent by the eyebrow. It was another case of Tedward knowing the person, but acting to stop something he considered dangerous by using the most efficient means available. Scott rose up, astonished, and said something like, "Man I oughta belt him one!" Tedward was grinning and staying just out of reach. I was amazed, and amused. I told my friend, "Think of it from his perspective, and you might agree that it was a very intelligent thing for him to do." Scott just grunted, but I thought I saw a gleam of admiration in his eye as he beheld Tedward in a new light.

Chapter 9

Now we come to a part of the story that Tedward himself might consider the most exciting of all. One of our lead horses, Molly, had a heart attack while Mike was riding her, with a full ride behind him. It was lucky Mike was the one on board, as he had rodeo skills to draw on. Molly suddenly turned off the trail and started running downhill like a locomotive. When he realized he couldn't stop her, Mike bailed off and rolled. He picked himself up, unhurt, and rushed back to where Molly had crashed on the ground. She was trembling and frothing at the mouth, and he quickly took off her bridle and loosened her cinch. She was dead in less than a minute. Thankfully this happened out of sight of the guests, who were waiting back up on the trail.

Mike led the ride the rest of the way home on foot, and Dave hopped on the small Caterpillar and went up to bury Molly. The ground was pretty steep and rocky, and he couldn't cover her very well. Later that evening, as we were playing cards and backgammon at the dinner table, we heard the coyotes yipping and yodeling from the direction Molly's body lay, and we knew they'd hit the mother lode.

I realized I hadn't seen Tedward for awhile. Suspicion dawned in my mind. Would he be up there with the coyotes, hoping to partake of the massive feast? I stood on the porch, calling and whistling, but there was no response. I went inside to continue beating the crap out of Dave—at backgammon, I mean.

An hour passed. I noticed the coyotes were quiet. Then Tedward suddenly appeared in the doorway, looking like some hideous apparition. He was literally covered with blood and gore! Gobbets of flesh hung off of him, and swung with his every move. He was wearing an ecstatic grin, like he'd just had the time of his life. Then the smell hit us. Dave and the other wranglers all jumped up at once and started hurrying down various hallways, away from the awful sight and stench. Dave, lumbering toward his room as fast as his creaky knees would let him, bellowed, "Good God, give the damn dog a bath!"

A similar scenario was repeated nightly for an entire week. Tedward seemed to have developed a sixth sense as to when I was thinking of catching him to tie him up. He would simply vanish, only to show up a few hours later, with the evidence of his debauchery plain for all to see. As I was hosing him off, he would often puke up enormous amounts of offal, some of which was even identifiable, such was his apparent greed in inhaling it.

But what I really wondered about was his position relative to the coyotes at the carcass. Was he, as an alleged honorary pack member, shoulder to shoulder with them while eating? Or did he have more of a subordinate Omega-like status, and hang back until the coyotes were finished? All I know is, he was certainly getting plenty of meat for himself. I would give my eyeteeth to have had a "coyotecam', or better yet, a 'Tedwardcam". This was a unique situation. How many dogs do you know that ate dinner with coyotes, and lived to tell about it? If Tedward had to sum up that experience, I can imagine him saying, "Best Party Ever!"

Chapter 10

There seemed to be no end to the mischief Tedward could get into. Seeing Dave shaking his head with a scowl on his face became an everyday thing. Now that he had added "Carrion-Craving Coyote Cohort" to his resume, I started a little game with myself, trying to predict what he'd do next to gain negative attention from our long-suffering bossman.

Tedward had always found great sport in chasing the Richardson's Ground Squirrels that had a colony on the far side of the packed-dirt parking lot. When the mood was on him, he would creep and lurk on the other side of the row of horses that were lined up at the 2 hitch rails, peering out between their legs at the squirrels, some of whom were usually outside their burrows nibbling the short grass. These rails were each about 20 feet long and a good 10 inches in diameter. They were nailed on stout supporting posts that stood a little over 3 feet high. We used quick-release knots on the horses' halter ropes. The horses would be saddled and tied to the rails, there to wait patiently until they were needed for a ride.

As I could see everything clearly from inside the reservation booth, I often watched Tedward at this game. I noticed that he usually timed his rush for the moments when there were at least 2 squirrels out in the open. I marveled at how none of the horses seemed particularly bothered by him brushing so close to their legs and tails. But sometimes when he took a bead on a squirrel and dashed for the colony, he would run right under a horse's belly—usually one that was at the end of one of the hitch rails. Even this didn't usually faze them too badly; sometimes one would give a little jump, and then settle back down. Others, caught dozing, would open their eyes suddenly, then relax when they realized it was only Tedward, up to his old tricks.

But one morning, a certain horse called Nugget happened to be tied at the end of the first rail. He was kind of an oddball; some days he seemed spooked by his own shadow. He'd bitten me on the wrist once when I wasn't quick enough to put the feed bag on him. That was the first and only time I ever beat a horse with his own feed bag. Anyway, things were pretty peaceful at first, as we led out the last few horses and tied them up, making about 12 horses to each of the 2 rails. Then we all relaxed a little, had some coffee, and waited for the first guests to arrive.

Tedward came trotting around the side of the barn, spotted several squirrels out of their burrows, and quickly took up a crouched position not far from Nugget's back legs. I watched him, holding my breath, as he shivered with excitement and then launched himself right under Nugget's belly. The horse immediately began to come unglued. His eyes bulged as he snorted and tried to rear up, but he couldn't because he was tied to the rail. Then he really lost it. The horse next to him pulled back hard on his halter rope, hoping to get away from the plunging, farting maniac. Other horses down the line were showing signs of nervousness, shifting their feet, pulling on their ropes, and rolling their eyes. I heard Chris say, "Oh, shit", as he came running out of the tackroom at my call, with the other wranglers close behind. This sort of thing could quickly get out of hand, with horses hurting each other in their state of panic.

Tedward, oblivious to the disaster-in-the-making behind him, was happily lunging to and fro after the squirrels. I watched in horror as the horses pulled the entire rail off its support posts. All their heads immediately dropped at the huge weight pulling downwards on their halter ropes. A total freak-out was imminent. But our guys saved the day. They bravely waded right in among the horses, quickly yanking free the halter rope knots, talking calmly to the them, saying things like, "Whoa now", and "Easy there, buddy". I started ferrying the jittery horses to the nearby rodeo arena, where they'd be able to walk it off until calm. A couple had been kicked by their neighbors, but there were no serious injuries.

As soon as I saw things coming under control, I whipped my head around quickly to see if Dave was anywhere in the vicinity. He wasn't, but I knew he would hear about what happened. I started rehearsing Tedward's defense in my mind. My main point would be that he had run under the horses many times, but it was just bad luck that it happened to be Nugget that was tied at the end of the rail today. I conjured up an embarrassing image of myself cringing and groveling and pleading with our boss not to ban Tedward from the entire county, as I knew he'd dearly love to do. But I got lucky—Dave had gone to pick up Julie, his visiting fiance, and was in a relatively benevolent frame of mind.

At dinner that night with Julie as our guest, he listened to the other wranglers' enthusiastic descriptions of the incident, with nary a frown on his face. (I thought to myself, wow, I hope he keeps this woman around the rest of the summer). He actually grinned now and then, acting like he was amused by the whole thing. Nevertheless, my dread would not totally leave me, and I still expected some dire consequence to befall both Tedward and me.

As I passed Dave in the hallway later that evening and glanced furtively at his face, he caught my eye, actually smiled a little and said, "Relax, Julie really enjoyed hearing about Tedward's latest exploits. Almost seems worth the aggravation!"*

Chapter 11

Other memories of horses doing strange things when frightened spring to mind. I believe we're going to have to time travel once more—yes, another B.T.F. (Before Tedward Flashback)—to 1974, the year of the great horse race.

On the front range of Colorado, thunderstorms can appear quickly during the summer afternoons. I remember getting caught several times on high trails, when the sky seemed to instantly turn black, large raindrops began pelting horses and riders, and the wind suddenly gusting and blowing manes and tails and women's long hair all over the place. I had to turn Joe back along the line of horses on our narrow mountain trails to help people get their slickers on. Joe would be eyeball to eyeball with the guests' horses as we squeezed by, and I would stop to untie the slicker—each saddle came with one tied on the back—and help the person put it on, with the wind flapping it all around. Joe was really good at keeping the other horses on an even keel, taking no guff, but not bullying them either. It goes against the grain for herd animals to confront each other face-on in close quarters like that. Sometimes a horse would toss his head and lay back his ears a little, but Joe would fix him with 'the eye of authority'—he held a pretty high position in the herd hierarchy—and the other horse would calm down and avert his gaze, thereby avoiding trouble.

If we were on our way down the mountain when a storm caught us, and if I had a small number of riders who I felt could stick on pretty well, I'd ask them if they wanted to "race the storm". I never once got a negative reply. It was especially exciting when the lightning started striking and the thunder booming and cracking, seemingly on top of us. Sometimes hairs from the horses' manes, and our own hair, would stand up in response to the electricity in the air around us. We would do a hurry-up jogtrot down the winding, rocky trails, and it was a rough ride, but people seemed to love it, especially the kids. We had a limit though: no one under 8 years old. This was wise, I thought, because sometimes even the adults, many of whom were not used to violent storms, rough terrain, wild animal noises, etc., could find themselves feeling a little uncertain at times.

As I may have mentioned before, traveling on a horse at anything other than a walk was frowned upon by the park rangers—in fact it was technically illegal. I never got caught in the act, but I did suffer a "retro-nab" one time. That curvy area not far from the barn, lined by aspens, was a great place to let the horses speed up a little. I forget how many riders I had behind me, but as Joe came swinging around one of the curves, I had to pull up quick to avoid a couple of senior ladies with their walking sticks. I know my eyes went wide when I saw them, and they were not too happy at having this large white animal startling them like that, right in their faces as it were. I apologized and continued on with my group as the old biddies, I mean the senior ladies, waited to the side.

When we got back to the barn after our 2-hour ride to Cub Lake, Chris and Jeff were wearing big smiles as I dismounted. After helping the guests off their horses and receiving their thank yous and goodbyes, I said, "Allright, what's up with you guys?" Jeff said, "Well, we heard that you almost ran over 2 little old ladies on the trail!" I tried to defend myself while those 2 goons practically had to hold each other up, they were laughing so hard. I guess it was kind of funny, but what was really killing them, as they finally managed to croak out, was that when the 2 ladies complained to Steve, our manager, they told him that my eyes flew wide open, that my horse was "out of control", and that they thought there should be "real cowboys" leading the rides, not young girls. More hoots and guffaws followed this statement, as I shook my head, humor mingling with disgust. If I only knew then that in what would seem like the blink of an eye, I would be an "old biddie" myself!

Chapter 12

We're still in 1974, at Moraine Park Stables in Rocky Mountain National Park, Colorado, one of the most beautiful areas on the face of the earth, in my not-so-humble opinion. The trail horses we worked with and that carried our "dudes" and ourselves up and down the mountains had pretty steady nerves. But, being horses, they would sometimes get a little goosey from time to time. I recollect one afternoon when the threatening clouds were getting closer, finally blocking out the sun, as those of us not on rides were raking the corrals. Suddenly a huge clap of thunder made us jump, and every single one of the 6 horses tied to the fence closest to us took a simultaneous shit. There were a few minutes of uncontrollable laughter before we were able to get busy with the shovels.

We all became pretty fanatic that summer about keeping the corrals spotless. We even used long-handled brushes on the packed dirt, because the ground was so uneven with rocks poking through everywhere, that just using the rake wouldn't get it totally clean. Our youngest wrangler, Danny, did take it to the extreme though. If he even saw a horse lift its tail, he'd grab a shovel, hustle over and stick it right under the horse's rump to catch the offerings in mid-drop. Some of the horses didn't appreciate the rather sharp edge of the shovel touching their keisters, and we had many a laugh at Danny's contortions to avoid their kicking back hooves.

Speaking of socially unacceptable bodily functions, Joe, my faithful buddy, had a marked propensity for passing gas. Everyone who knew me just had to say it: he was the perfect horse for me. Why they would say this I have no idea. But this particular talent of Joe's would sometimes display itself inadvertently on rides, almost always getting some sort of reaction from the guests, as most of them hadn't been around horses that much, and were rather surprised at the loud, gunshot-like reports when they—meaning the horses—broke wind.

Just where the gravel road left off and the actual trail to Cub Lake began, there was a little place where the ground went down and then right up again. Most horses would naturally want to break into a trot right there. If the lead horse on a ride did so, every horse following would too. One day I had a full ride of 15 with 2 kids behind me, ages 8 and 10, with their parents just behind them. As usual it was an incredible summer morning in the Rockies, with sunshine, green leaves fluttering, and birds singing. There was congenial conversation up and down the line as we came to that little downslope. Most times I would allow Joe to jog down and up it, and I did so again, trusting that the kids and everyone else could handle it. But what made this time different was that Joe, with every beat of his hooves at the trot, let loose a thunderous fart.

The high-pitched screeching noises coming out of the kids' mouths made me unable to turn around to make sure they were still in their saddles, because I knew I would not be able to keep from joining them. I didn't want their parents and the other guests to think that we Moraine Park wranglers were a bunch of potty-humor-loving lowlifes. How I controlled myself I don't know, especially when one guy in the back hollered, "Guess that horse had beans for lunch!"

Back to horses getting scared: One time coming back from Fern Lake, my riders and I got a little "awakener" as we were passing the campground that was not far from our stables. (The very same campground the rangers evacuated later that summer when they found a white-footed deer mouse with a flea that was carrying bubonic plague. Interesting that they didn't bother to evacuate the wranglers living next door at the stables—hello!) I knew the guests were looking forward to getting off their horses and resting their backsides, as this was a 4-hour ride. I was half-asleep and I think Joe was too, when suddenly there was the sound of running hoofbeats, coming from behind. Mystified, I turned and saw the back half of my ride in a virtual horse race, rapidly catching up to those of us in the front, with their riders wide-eyed and hanging on to their saddle horns. Luckily no one fell off, but I couldn't figure out what in heck was causing it. Then I saw a large, white bear-like 4-legged critter in the rear, galloping gaily. It was a Great Pyrenees, that had apparently escaped from some campers. Since dogs weren't allowed in the campground, I don't know how they snuck that critter in, he was downright enormous. I imagined the horses yelling to each other, "It's a bear, run for your lives!"

I myself once put the fear of God into a horse named Funny Face. This was a big, gentle, likeable horse, with a crooked blaze down his nose—hence the name—who only had one fault: he was slower than sin on a Sunday. No matter where we put him in the line of horses, he would lag like a mofo. If he had horses behind him, he would hold them all up as he dawdled down the trail, deliberately placing one hoof in front of the other, taking his sweet time. With our manager always breathing down our necks about getting the rides out and back on time, this could cause some stress. The wrangler was constantly having to wait for Funny Face and whoever was following him to catch up. Most of the guests could not bring themselves to kick a horse's sides too hard, not being used to it and all. I even sometimes let the guest riding him borrow my crop, and it was amusing to see them tap-tapping Funny Face timidly on the butt. I'd tell them to give him a good whack, but they just couldn't do it.

One day I finally had it. Funny Face was last in line, and at one point on the Beaver Meadows trail, I looked around and swear to God he was a quarter mile back. Why his rider didn't call out, I don't know. I galloped Joe back to him, swung around Funny Face's rear, told the rider to hang on, and walloped him a good one. He really stepped out

Jeff and horses, Moraine Park corrals

Alaska Railroad train, heading south toward Anchorage

then, in fact for a second there I thought he might actually break into a trot. I broke my crop with that whack, which I took alot of ribbing for, back at the barn.

Next time I had Funny Face on one of my rides, I walked up to him, showed him my replacement crop, and gave him a stern lecture, telling him to remember last time, and don't make me lay one on you in front of God and everybody, etc. He really seemed to get it, as he never lagged on one of my rides after that.

I could see why the horses would get tired of carrying humans—many of whom were frankly on the large side—up and down the same trails day after day. Even though I would urge my riders to keep a third of their weight in the stirrups, thereby taking some of the strain off the horses' backs and kidneys, they just couldn't or wouldn't do it for very long. So some, like Funny Face, developed little ways to rebel. Totally understandable.

A few had more amusing techniques to show how tired they were of the same old steep, hot trails. On the Cub Lake ride, most of the horses would step a ways into the lake when we reached it and paused to rest a bit. A certain bay mare named Cheetah used to take this even farther; she would step out until she was about knee deep in the water and lay down, rider and all. You really had to watch her closely to prevent this from happening, because most dudes didn't have the presence of mind to firmly steer her back toward the shore, let alone step off her as she went down. After the first couple of times she did this, we stuck to putting experienced riders on her, and eventually she became Ella's lead horse. (Ella was our wrangler from Florida). The first time Cheetah "went swimming" was on my ride, and I watched as she waded out with her clueless rider holding the reins way too long, allowing her to get out to where it was a couple of feet deep. When she started vigorously pawing at the water with one front hoof, everyone laughed including the middle-aged man sitting on her. I turned my head to say something to someone else, and I heard a shout and when I looked back, there was Cheetah, lolling on her side in the lake, saddle and blanket getting soaked, and the guest standing beside her, up to his knees, still holding one rein.

It's just so hard not to laugh when everybody around you is busting up. I had to give in to it as I rode over there and waved my crop towards Cheetah's rear end, while telling the guest to step back. She was lounging like a bathing beauty—the horse, not the guest—eyes half closed, obviously relishing the feel of the cool water on her skin after the steep trail up. She looked so happy I almost wanted to let her continue for awhile, but I knew it wasn't doing the saddle any good. She lunged to a stand, shook like a dog, and I led her back to the shore where her rider was able to mount easily by standing on a rock. Once we were headed home, Cheetah was a perfect lady.

Most of the horses were gentle and even downright friendly—easy to handle on the ground and in the saddle. There were one or two exceptions though; a handsome dapple-grey gelding named Shotgun comes to mind. The only one that could really ride him was our manager Steve. Danny thought he could handle him, but after Shotgun reared up with him and went over backwards and crashed, nearly cracking Danny's skull on the corral fence, he had to admit defeat.

We had what was called a saddling chute at that stables, the only one I've ever seen. It was a roofed-over mini-barn type thing, with a door on each end big enough for one horse to come through. You could fit 3 horses in at a time, nose to tail. On one side there was the grain chute, feed bags, curry combs and brushes. On the other, larger side, there were the saddles, pads, bridles, and more combs and brushes. The horses were funneled into position by the way the rails were positioned in the corral. Since they wanted their grain, by the time we would stumble half-asleep down to the barn at 6 a.m., the horses would be standing in line like kids waiting to get on a ride at the fair. Inside the chute, there were 6-inch diameter rails about 3 and ½ feet high running lengthwise, the same width apart as the doorways. Horizontal bars were slid in front of the foremost horse and in back of the rearmost to keep them in place. With 2 wranglers on the left side, one to fill the feed bag and put it on the horse's head, the other to start brushing, and 2 or 3 on the right, brushing, then putting pads and saddles on, with the bridle tied to the saddle horn, it was like an assembly line. If the horses were finished being tacked but were still eating, we would let them out of the chute with their feed bags on, and collect them later. It was amusing to see them propping the feed bags on the corral fences or even each other, to get at those last bits at the bottom. It was a very efficient system.

Once in awhile a horse would act up in there, which was a little hairy, it being such close quarters. One time I dropped a brush on the grain side, right next to Shotgun standing there on the other side of the rail. When I bent over to pick it up, I heard a loud "thunk". When I raised up, the other wranglers' faces were pale. I asked what the matter was, and Jeff said that just as I bent over, Shotgun reared up, and when he came down his hoof hit the rail on my side and almost slid down off it and onto my head.

On the other end of the spectrum, we had one horse named Cricket that was extremely friendly. In fact he was so friendly that Chris said he thought maybe he wasn't "wrapped too tight". He used to let us climb on his back and sit on him—Cricket, not Chris—when he was laying down in the corral. We could also sit on the ground and lean back against his tummy; which not one of the other horses would have allowed, not even Joe.

Speaking of Joe, and horses being spooked, I remember a certain encounter with a lightning bolt when I was riding above timberline one time. Joe was pretty reliable in almost every trail situation you could dream up. I had ridden him over downed timber covered with snow, and he never hesitated, he just carefully but confidently put each foot down and let it either balance on or slide over the unseen logs without getting upset. We'd ridden through fast-running streams above his knees and hocks, no problem. One trail with enormous mud holes and no way to get off to the sides gave me 2 hours of stomach aches, but Joe just plowed and plunged through every one without turning a hair, his belly and legs totally black afterwards. But on one high-altitude switchback with a storm starting to engulf us, I saw the lightning hit about 50 feet up the mountain. Joe twirled like a ballerina, and headed right back down the trail. I didn't argue. He had placed his feet perfectly in that little maneuver, which was awesome because one misstep there would have meant the kind of tumble you don't recover from.

One thing that did scare Joe was a veterinarian coming towards him with a needle in his hand. I used a vet in Estes Park that I always thought of as a gentle, mild-mannered sort of guy, until he tried to give Joe a shot once and got thrown to the ground. As I watched my horse galloping for the nearest set of trees, my ears were subjected to some of the worst language I ever heard. So much for Mr. Nice Guy.*

We had a medium-sized palomino mare at Moraine Park named High Note. She had low withers, which made us have to cinch the saddle really tight to keep it from twisting on her. On the Fern Lake Trail one day, I heard somebody call me from the back of the ride, and when I turned to look, the lady that was riding High Note was sitting at an impossible angle, but not really looking concerned. I climbed off Joe and made my way back along the rocky edge of the trail. It wasn't a good place for an inexperienced rider to dismount, so I braced myself and told the lady, on the count of 3, wrench your body to the right. That's when it would have been handy to have a "real cowboy" around, as I could hardly budge the damn thing. Luckily High Note had a very placid temperament. Just to imagine trying it on Shotgun made me want to duck and run. We had to do it 3 times, and finally she was sitting almost upright. My back was sore for a week.

When it became apparent that I could always get the better of Chris and Jeff when it came to gas-giving—and I mean verbal gas, not the other kind—being typical guys, they would eventually have to resort to physical means to get even. I would fire off one too many insults, and Chris would turn to Jeff and say, "I've had just about enough. How about you?" and Jeff would say, "Oh yes, I've had about all I can take." That was the signal for the war games to begin, and I had to watch my every move. Those 2 varmints would plot and plan how and when they were going to grab me to throw me in the horse trough. It usually took both of them to do it, as I could outrun them both, and was pretty strong for my size, which was about 115 lbs. soaking wet. (Double it and that's about what I weigh now, Lord have mercy). In fact Jerry, who worked for the Van Horns (the owners), and who famously tipped the front-end loader on its side one day while trying to shovel manure with it, tried to wrestle me over the rail in the saddle chute one day, and he couldn't do it. Thereafter he referred to me as a "stout little girl". Chris and Jeff got alot of mileage out of that one.

A bit about the local wildlife: we saw quite a few elk, especially early on. We had a late snow that caused trail closures for a couple of days. We, the wranglers, all went riding together, Jeff galloping ahead on Skip, making sure to dump snow on those of us following, by grabbing the loaded tree limbs as he passed, and letting them go at the last second, the rotter. I got an inkling then of Joe's drive to overtake any horse running in front of him, and had my hands full holding him back. When we saw a small herd of elk on the trail up ahead, did we slow down, as per park rules, so as not to bother the wildlife? Heck no, Jeff took one look and he and Skip tore off after them, the rest of us doing our best to keep up. I guess no rangers saw us, because I didn't hear anything about it later.**

There was a section near the beginning of the Beaver Meadows Trail where twice I had wild critters parallel my ride. First was a golden eagle, who with his large wingspan, had just enough room to glide at saddle level through the ponderosas, electrifying my riders. It was a moment of stillness as he passed, then everyone started talking and exclaiming. A few weeks after that it was a coyote, who jogged along about 40 feet abreast of Joe and me, not looking at us or acknowledging us in any way, yet keeping company until the trail steepened and he veered off. Another thrill for my guests, who speculated all over the place as to why the coyote would show himself to us like that. I had to remind them that this was a national park, where there was no hunting allowed, and that the animals didn't have to be so afraid of human presence. (Except for a certain small group of elk).

On that same trail, which led way out in the valley between the 2 glacial moraines, a wrangler from the year before had gone to sleep on his horse and fallen off right in front of his guests. Leading rides a couple of times in Beaver Meadows on warm summer afternoons, after staying up late, talking and laughing with my co-workers, I saw how it could happen. Man, talk about embarrassing. I don't know how we avoided it, frankly. Oh, and God forbid I was even 5 minutes late getting out of my bunk in the morning; Chris would appear at the door with a glass of cold water, which he would pour right on my face. That right there proves there's such a thing as miracles, because after all these years, and all the pranks and harpoon jokes, we are still friends.

Chapter 13

We're going to stay in B. T.—Before Tedward—time, and take a little trip to Jackson Hole, Wyoming. After our manager Steve got fired, in part for yelling at us in front of the guests, but mainly for sitting on his ass when he should have been working, and after the 3 awesome days that we wranglers ran the whole place with nary a hitch, the Van Horns sold the concession to a man named Rex. Now doesn't that sound like a good name for a villain? Either that or a dog...anyway it was common knowledge that he'd let some of his horses starve on a range near Craig a couple of winters before. We did not want to work for this asshole, so we all quit and headed up to Jackson. My first memory of that trip was on Highway 80 in southern Wyoming, with me driving Chris's truck, Chris riding shotgun, Jeff driving Danny's truck with Danny riding shotgun, and Jeff yelling at us to come closer so he could pass a gallon jug of water to Chris through the windows of our trucks which were hurtling down the road, one in each lane, at about 75 miles an hour. I weenied out and wouldn't do it, and I had to take some harsh ribbing for my chicken-heartedness.

The landscape was pretty bleak for a long ways, but we did see a small herd of pronghorns out on the dry plains. Around Pinedale it started looking better, as the land started to rise and become more forested. When you drop into the "Hole", it is stunning. The Tetons rise up 7,000 feet out of the flat valley floor, which itself is around 7,000 feet elevation. It was all different shades of green, with the Snake River winding through it. It was the 3rd of July, 1974, and we camped at the foot of Snow King Mountain near the edge of town that first night. The next day we became acquainted not just with the elk in the nearby refuge, but also with the mosquitos. That was our first task, to purchase a large can of Cutter's Insect Repellant. Chris would squeeze his eyes shut and spray it directly on his face. I noticed that walking through downtown Jackson, which was crowded with both tourists and locals, that the predominant smell was not perfume, aftershave, or sweat—it was Cutter's.

We spent a good part of that first day trying to find a motel room for the night. As you can imagine, the town was packed pretty full, there being a 4th of July rodeo and fireworks and chili cook-offs and all manner of holiday doings. As the afternoon wore on, the guys were getting discouraged. I was determined not to lose hope, however, and eventually scored a room over a bar. Noisy? You bet, but mosquito-free.

I have a vivid mental picture of Chris standing outside the motel with a blanket over his head, smoking a cigar. He said this was more effective than Cutter's. All I can say is it sure caused the rest of us to stay away from him.

By the end of the very next day we all had jobs. I got hired as a wrangler at Warm Springs Ranch, on the border of Grand Teton National Park. (The land was eventually sold and now belongs to the Park). Chris, Jeff and Danny all got hired to work hauling and distributing hay for the elk refuge. On a mutual day off, Chris and I decided to take an English riding lesson from a reputable instructor in the area. We both had ridden English before we came to Colorado. This teacher was so great, the total opposite of the poisonous old hag that gave me lessons when I was 9. I was on a young, somewhat green Thoroughbred mare, and we got into a good flow and were going over jumps and it really felt right. The instructor was yelling things like, "Looks good!" and "Nice one!". He even asked me at one point if I'd ever considered being a professional rider. Wow, that was a great compliment. Jeff, who would not even consider riding English, was leaning on the rail watching us. His favorite part was when the teacher told me to let my hips drop more with the horse's stride at the walk, so it wouldn't look like I was "belly dancing". I was teased about that for the rest of the week, at least. Ahh, Jeff, if you could only see my "boiler" now. *

On another day off, we went rafting. The guys went for the white-water trip, but I opted for the slower, more serene and restful wildlife-watching tour. I saw my first beaver, my first moose, and my first bald eagle on that trip. It was worth the gas I took for being too chicken to dare the other. In the evenings, we sometimes went into town for dinner. Every single restaurant or gift shop we walked into had multiple animal heads on the walls. It was a little unsettling, having a moose with glass eyeballs looming over you as you ate your steak. Seriously, the people up there are very much into killing wildlife. The hardware store had a whole pyramid of pronghorn heads. And I remember a large outdoor archway made up of nothing but elk antlers. Bizarre.

You've heard of Cowboy Bob, perhaps. Well, at Warm Springs Ranch, I worked with a cowboy named Bob. He was a pretty good guy, and we got along well. I couldn't get over how the horses would lay down at the hitch rail with their saddles on. The first time I saw this, I started clapping my hands and waving my arms to get them to stand up, and Bob said, "That's okay, they can lay there if they want". Allrighty then. The other thing was, there were tons of shitpiles around and Bob seemed in no hurry to pick them up. This I insisted upon, however, and he would lean against the tackroom door with the ever-present toothpick in his mouth, shaking his head at my eagerness to "tidy up", as he called it.

On the first day, he handed me some wirecutters to put in my sad-dlebag. I asked why we needed to carry them, and he said, you never know when you might have to cut through a fence. This sounded a bit strange, but what the hey, this was Wyoming. It turned out I needed them that very day. In the morning Bob led the way on his horse, and he had recommended a smallish sorrel named Stoutheart for me. What a great little horse. He had a great personality; he was smart, perky, and willing. I seriously thought of buying him to keep Joe company.

Bob showed me where the trail was—the only trail—and commented that it was easy to get screwed up on the top of the hill, and miss the opening in the fence. I told him no worries, I'd just spent the first part of the summer on much longer and more complex trails than this. None of the ranch guests went riding until the afternoon. I took out a family of four, and as we were riding along, I looked down and both of my legs were covered with mosquitos. I had put repellant everywhere else except on my jeans, which I figured were thick enough that the little bloodsuckers couldn't penetrate. It looked like I was wearing black fuzzy chaps.

The ride went well until we got up on top, and darned if I could find the blasted opening, and had to cut the fence. Then of course, after we all walked our horses through, I had to wire it back up, which isn't easy, even for a stout little girl. I could see down to the barn area from several points on that hilltop, and I hoped Bob hadn't been watching me cast around for the right way to go.

We got back down, the guests were happy with their horses, me, and the ride in general, and Bob didn't say anything until they had left and we were loosening the cinches. Then he looked at me over the back of the horse he was working on, shifted the toothpick to the other side of his mouth, grinned a little and said, "I saw you flub up there on top."

A few days later I was tying a horse to one of the rails and just when I finished with the knot he pulled back hard. I turned my head toward where he was looking, and there was a badger, poking his head out of a hole in the bank about 40 feet away—the first one I'd ever seen in the wild. Without thinking, I yelled to Bob, "Hey, check out the badger!" He saw it and said, "I'm going to get that sonofabitch", and hurried to the tackroom. I had a sinking feeling in my stomach. Bob then came out with a long pole with a hook on one end, went over to the burrow, and started ramming the pole in there at various angles. I was horrified and yelled at him to stop. He said, no, that the owner had told him to kill every badger he saw, because horses can break their legs in their holes. I thought maybe he wouldn't catch it, because I knew they dig pretty long tunnels, but as I turned back to the horse to adjust his saddle, I heard a new sound. I couldn't help looking, and sure enough, there was Bob, beating the badger to death with the pole. Thank goodness the badger itself was hidden from my sight by the grass. I couldn't speak to Bob the rest of the day—it just made me sick. Later I saw one of the owner's 3-year-old twins, dragging the dead badger around the yard by a foot, the other hand up to her mouth, sucking her thumb. Oy.

Our next day off we drove up into Yellowstone, to the West Thumb area. I remember walking through a sparse forest and there on the ground was a steaming water hole about 2 feet across, and inside were rocks of amazingly bright shades of green, yellow and turquoise. We were going to take a look at Jenny Lake on the way back, until we saw a huge cloud of mosquitoes hovering right over the walkway. When we got back in town, I was riding shotgun in Danny's truck, which had a unique feature: a genuine P.A. system. We stopped at a light and there was a cop on our right hand. Inspiration struck, and I grabbed the mike and said loudly, "Hey, you pig!" Danny's face went totally white. After I finished laughing, I assured him that I hadn't pressed the button.

Danny decided to head back to southern California; we were sorry to see him go. He was pretty good company for a whippersnapper. (He was 17; Chris and Jeff were 19, and I was the old-timer of the group, at 21.) Plus he was supposed to be the 3rd member of their team at the

Wild Horse Race event the following Saturday. Later the same afternoon, Chris and Jeff stopped by the ranch and Chris said, "Well, we're all signed up for the rodeo!" I said, "So who's going to be your 3rd person?" and he said, "You are."

I got a stomach-ache just thinking about it. We'd seen this event. You basically have an unbroke horse that you have to rope, saddle and put a halter on and ride him to the other end of the arena before the others. One horse we saw never even stopped running as he neared the 6-foot fence, he just leaped up and crashed right into it. I was adamant, there was no way I was going to do it. But those varmints almost had me talked into it, until fate intervened, in the form of a romantic snafu. Jeff had been hinting that he might go visit a girl he knew in Cody. Since Jeff and I had been pretty much a couple for a few weeks, I found this upsetting. Then when one of us asked him when he might go, he said, "Cody's coming here." That did it. I decided to leave with 2 of the ranch guests who'd offered me a ride to California a day or 2 before.

When I walked into the tackroom and told Bob I was quitting, I could tell he was disappointed. He kind of looked off in the distance, shifted his toothpick and said, "Well, if you got to, you got to." I was hearing an inner voice in my head saying no, don't do it, but did I listen? Of course not. I wouldn't exactly say my heart was broken, it was more my pride that was injured. Not listening to that inner voice started a really annoying train of bad luck that lasted the rest of the summer.

Alaskan moose

Chris's wolverine

Chapter 14

The 2 nurses from New York City that had offered me a ride to San Francisco turned out to be a couple of righteous bitches. At first they were nice, offering to put some of their bags on top of their not-too-roomy car, so I could put my stuff inside. But about 10 miles along the freeway, there was a little mishap, with one suitcase falling off the rack and everything inside ending up all over the road. They pulled over and we dashed around picking it all up—not too much traffic, luckily—and they were suddenly all pissed at me, for taking up so much room. (Even though I wasn't the one who did a lousy job of tying the stuff on the rack). They were going to leave me right there on the side of the freeway! I guess you just can't trust a New Yorker, to quote Chris, who was from New York, but "not the city", as he made a point of telling everyone. Anyway I talked them into taking me to the nearest Greyhound station, and I had just enough money to pay for my ticket. I recall the gorgeous purple tones of the Ruby Mountains in Nevada as we passed through around sunset on the second evening.

I stopped in the bay area and then traveled to the central coast to check out horse jobs. I just missed getting a job at Gainey Arabians; the owner had hired someone the day before. Bad luck item #2. Then, I landed a job at a saddlebred farm in Los Olivos. It didn't start for a week or so, so I went back to the bay area, and found out Chris and Jeff, who'd just been to the World's Fair in Seattle, had passed through trying to find me, but were now headed back to Colorado. That's #3. Then, I got mononucleosis: #4. Finally, I made it back to Los Olivos and started the job, which proved to be a little too much for my capabilities. These horses were hot-blooded, fed alot of grain, kept in stalls except for exercise once a day, and were way taller than all our Colorado trail horses—and they definitely were not gentle. There was only one, a black mare named Hobart, who I liked and trusted.

I was doing things like lungeing young stallions, hitching up fractious mares to buggies, shampooing horses whose withers I could barely reach, and other scary stuff. I also hated the things they did to make the horses look good in the show ring, like keep chains on their fetlocks at night, so every time they moved their feet, they would get a little knock on the coronet (the band of tissue just above the hoof), and it made them want to pick up their feet quickly. And cutting the muscles in the back of the tails and keeping braces on them, so their tails would have that little curve at the top. And putting ginger in their anuses, which was an irritant, making them act just a little bit more excited than normal. And letting their feet grow too long and putting heavy shoes on them, to extend their stride. Talk about how to make a horse into something it's not.

So the saddlebred ranch was bad luck thing #5. I was rescued by my sister and brother-in-law, and spent a little time in L.A. with them, but the Rockies and Joe were calling me. And the worm of luck was about to turn.

Chapter 15

So we're still in this really long Before-Tedward flashback, and it's now October of 1974, and we're once again in beautiful Estes Park, Colorado. I got Joe back from Jerry, who wanted more money than we agreed on for keeping him over the summer, because he claimed someone offered him $600 for him. Never trust a redneck you hardly know, even if he's fun to joke around with. Joe was very happy to see me, whinnying and running up to me like always. But I was dismayed to see that all 4 of his legs had wire cuts. I guess it was a little too much trouble for Jerry to remove the discarded rolls of barbed wire from that small pasture.

I believe it was Mr. Brownfield, owner of Brownfield's Saddlery—a very nice man who enjoyed talking and had a good sense of humor—that gave me a recommendation for a temporary place to put Joe, at the Flower's place west of town. It was a good-sized corral with trees for shade and room to get up a gallop, if Joe was so inclined. And it was the Flowers, a delightful older couple that had lived in Estes for many years, who told me to go down the road and talk to Mrs. Oldham, because she and her husband just might need a caretaker for their property over the winter.

I did just that, and Mrs. O. and I hit it off immediately. The property, as I have already described, was a delight, with the aspens and ponderosas, and the charming little cabins—one main one, and 3 guest cabins, plus a couple of small outbuildings. Very homey, with that fantastic view out the back window of the main cabin. For a measly $60 a month, I lived there from October until the next May. Looking back, it was the best place I've ever lived, outside of my parents' house.

I think it was that same month, October, that I started working for Marion Burns, a sled-dog racer who lived in the mountains west of Boulder. I helped her around her place, doing everything from mucking out horse stalls to helping her get her young Siberian Huskies used to pulling sleds in harness. She had a new litter of pups, and she agreed to give me one if I did a certain amount of work. I think it was around late November or early December when I brought Nikki home. She was about 4 months old then.

Meanwhile, the first job I had in Estes was at Nicky's Restaurant. It was the first time I'd ever been a waitress. I made friends with a girl around my age, Suzanne. We both ended up migrating to jobs at the Ramada Inn, a little east of town. That place was the setting for the most fun I've ever had at a paying job in my life.

There just happened to be a great group of young people working there, and the kitchen boss was amazing, truly a decent human being and funny to boot. His name was Dino, and if every boss was like him, the world would sure be a much happier place. He encouraged us when it got really busy, saying things like, "You're doing great!", and "Only 45 minutes left to go!" I never heard him use a harsh word, yet everyone wanted to do their best for him. Although I've had a few really good bosses during my working life—and yes, Dave, I guess I can include you in that list—nobody ever equalled Dino.

My 4 favorite people during that time were Beth, also a waitress, and her sister Karen, and Kathy and Flossie, who had second jobs at another nice restaurant in town, Rock Acres. We all got to be friends so quickly, like sometimes happens when you work together, and we loved visiting each other's houses and hanging out, listening to music and eating, playing guitars, etc. Kathy in particular was a fantastic cook, and threw these great parties. She and Flossie had an enormous collection of records. (That's record albums, for you whippersnappers). And about 3 years later, Flossie ended up marrying Jeff, my old flame!

Karen was the musician of the group, and she is still playing gigs in western Colorado, her band's name is "Collage". She says playing with and for other people keeps her young. (Some of us are have aged more gracefully than others; Chris's most current nickname for me is "Shortround", which may give you a hint as to which one of the old gang is the least "in shape".)

But the most fun thing I did that winter was cross-country ski, and my favorite ski buddy was Beth. We both had a bit of the old competitive drive going, and it used to tick me off that she was so darned fearless on skis. She had been skiing practically since birth, plus she was athletic by nature. Steep, oddly-angled backcountry slopes were nothing to her. She would haul ass down treacherous trails, with me meekly snow-plowing behind her, cursing her all the way.

My favorite was our trip to Centennial Wyoming. We just had to pick the coldest 2 nights in January. Beth's friends Winston and Arnie accompanied us; in fact the trip may have been their idea, because I believe they were the ones that knew about the backcountry trapper's cabin that was our destination. I remember driving a few hours, then taking a ski-lift up to the top of a mountain, me holding Nikki, who was then about 6 months old, in my lap, and then taking off from there on our cross-country skis, cruising around the mostly gentle slopes, looking for the cabin and not finding it. At dusk, we saw an old beat up lean-to, and decided to camp there for the night. And what a cold, windy, miserable night it was! Beth and I both had summer bags (down bags rated to summer temperatures only), and we each were not aware of the other's suffering. It was one of the longest nights of my life.

But the next morning dawned bright and beautiful, and we set off with high hopes. The sun on the new snow was sparkling, the sky was blue, and there was no wind. We were following a small creek for awhile and I heard bird song, but I thought, no—it's winter, there aren't any birds that would sing like that now, just the nutcrackers and jays with their harsh squawks. But then I heard it again, and asked the others, who told me it was a dipper, John Muir's water ouzel, and that it sings all winter long! This became one of my favorite birds, in part because, although plain in appearance, it is at home in all 3 elements. It dips and bobs near the water—some say this is so it can see in between the reflections—then dives in and walks on the bottom, wings half cocked, probing under stones for aquatic insects. Their nests are little hobbit-like hovels, built by the streams. And their song is a delight for the ears.

We came to a long, steep downhill, which the 2 guys and Beth tackled before I did, making deep tracks in the powder. This made it almost impossible to take the hill slowly, as by the time it was my turn, it was like one long groove, with no room to do my usual snowplow maneuver. I also wasn't used to skiing with a backpack. I stood poised at the top of the hill, while the others waited below, Beth planting herself sideways right at the bottom and looking up at me with an eager expression on her face. I knew she was aware of my fears of going fast downhill, and she was plainly looking forward to the show. She wasn't disappointed. I held it together for about the first quarter of the way down, then as my speed increased, I got nervous and began to stiffen up. I lost it, regained it, then lost it again for good, doing a monumental face-plant about two-thirds of the way down. When I extricated my head and wiped out the snow that was jammed behind my glasses and down my neck, I saw and heard just what I expected: Beth bent double at the waist, holding herself up with her ski poles, bellowing with laughter.

We found the cabin, and I remember Beth bending over to scoop snow to melt for water to cook our dinner in, and Nikki was barking and dashing at her big derriere sticking up, in those black ski pants, imagining it to be some sort of prey. Beth said, "Caryl, if she bites me......!" with a threatening look, as I urged Nikki on, saying "Sic 'em!", etc. We were so tired that evening that we let the guys cook dinner, and freeze-dried rice and beef never tasted so good. We couldn't get the wood stove to work, and doubled up on the 2 cots in our sleeping bags. The next day

Beth told me privately that during the night when she turned over, there was Winston, ready and waiting to plant one on her.

That's all I recall from the trip itself; when we got back to Estes, Lola, the head waitress, fired me for being late one too many times, and when I walked into the main cabin at the Oldham's, it was 32 degrees inside (below zero outside)—the gauge was apparently already frozen when I checked it before we left—no more propane! I believe Karen, Beth's sister was with me that evening as we built a huge fire—thank goodness for the fireplace—and cuddled up with the dogs, drank some wine and tried to play guitar with our cold fingers.

Lola hired me back a week later. I guess she couldn't live without the one waitress that would give her a hard time. She actually snuck up on me in the kitchen one day and stuffed frozen frog legs down the neck of my uniform. I let out a shriek to wake the dead, that the hotel manager heard in the front lobby. I was told later that he started to jump up from his desk, then said, "Oh, it's probably Caryl", and sank back down.

Lola was always hoping to catch any of her waitresses doing something wrong, such as filching the cherry cheesecake that was kept in the small 'fridge in the coffee shop waitress station, a constant temptation. One time Beth came around the corner carrying dishes and saw me quickly pulling my hand out of the 'fridge and stuffing a bite of cheesecake in my mouth. She quickly set down her load and in a hoarse whisper commanded, "Oh my God, gimme some of that!" and as I backed away to give her room, saying "Yes, Boss", sarcastically, we both suddenly burst into uncontrollable laughter. That was when she informed me that my mouth assumed the shape of a heart when I laughed hard, whereas I noticed that hers was shaped more like a flower pot. Just then the door from the kitchen began to swing open, and we both high-tailed it into the lobby and around through the dining room, trying unsuccessfully to stifle ourselves.

Another thing that drove Lola to distraction was my habit of eating small amounts throughout my shift. Since I was running and skiing alot in those days, I was pretty much in fighting trim, and could eat as much and as often as I wanted. (Sigh.) Lola would say, "Caryl, why can't you sit down and eat one meal and then be done, like a normal person?" She was fond of posting lists of rules for her waitresses, and one of the commands read, "No Grazing! Caryl, this means you."

I sometimes worked the dining room with Kathy, the owner of the afore-mentioned Rocky. She was almost as good as Beth at initiating hilarity in the workplace. On Sundays we were working a champagne brunch, and the conservative local ladies in their hats and gloves were taking over the dining room. We would serve the champagne with peach halves floating in the glasses. I came into the waitress station from the kitchen and there was Kathy, with the magnum bottle hefted up high, taking a swig. I was aghast. I said, "What, are you nuts? Lola's in the kitchen!" She just lowered the bottle, gave a little burp and said, "Here you go—hold out a coffee cup." She expertly filled it just the right amount to leave enough room for a peach half. After indulging ourselves during that shift, some of the ladies noticed their eggs bene- dict and french toast were a bit late in arriving, and their waitresses uncommonly cheerful.*

Speaking of breakfast, Suzanne, who stayed with me at the Oldham's for 3 weeks, used to like pancakes, and we would enjoy them in the glassed-in dining room of the main cabin. Joe used to climb the 4 steps onto the porch and hover around the door, watching us as we ate, wait- ing for his bites, which he would take right off the fork. (He would also drink Coke out of a bottle, and ate turkey on Thanksgiving.) By the time Nikki was 6 months old, she had discovered that it was fun to harass large mammals. She and Joe used to have what I called "porch wars". Nikki would sit at the top of the steps and stare at Joe as he approached, sometimes growling and lifting her lips to show off her wicked-looking fangs. Joe would usually just lay his ears back and keep coming. Size does matter, after all.

My 2 favorite establishments in town were MacDonald's Bookstore and Diamond Jim's. The bookstore is still there, and still owned and run by the same wonderful lady, Paula. In the 3 years I lived off and on in Estes, we had some great talks, and she hired me to do some odd jobs for her, knowing how hard it was for us "youngsters" to make ends meet in the winters. Diamond Jim's used to be an old hunting lodge higher up in the national park, and they brought it down piece by piece, I forget what year, and made a tavern out of it. It was hands down the best place to go for music and dancing. I remember sitting on one of the couches, by the wood-burning stove one night with my friend Mike, and a full pitcher of beer came sailing over our heads and crashed on the floor in front of us. People used to climb on and hang from the rafters over the dancers. It was a blast. I believe the building is still there.

I remember a nice old lady named Grace (anybody over 50 was an old lady in those days), that picked me up hitchhiking between downtown and the Oldham's. When I invited her in and introduced her to Joe and Nikki, she was thrilled, saying she loved animals. We became friends, and I noticed she was quick to size up my temporary roomate, Wendy, a former co-worker from Nicky's Restaurant, referring to her as having a "push-button smile." That was one of my mistakes, letting that skank (Wendy, not Grace) and her pimply-faced boyfriend stay with me. When they departed for greener pastures in Bend, Oregon, they stole a bunch of my albums and left me with a phone bill. And that was not long after I helped her up and encouraged her after she took a hard crash on her skis at Monarch. That's gratitude for you.

Joe and Nikki were good company that winter. I used to ride Joe through town and up over a small hill to get to Beth's house. The morning after I'd ridden him home through a snowstorm around 9 p.m., I waited on a few of the local cops at the coffee shop. "I saw you riding right down the middle of Elkhorn Avenue last night", one of them said. I replied, "Were you thinking of giving me a ticket?" He shook his head as he shoveled a forkful of eggs into his mouth. "Naw. You weren't even close to the speed limit."

Chapter 16

Now we come to the spring of 1975, still pre-Tedward. It's a nice warm day and I'm in my swimsuit, doing dishes in the Oldham's kitchen. In saunters a large, rangey cowboy and takes off his hat. He's so glad to see me he's almost at a loss for words, although he manages to scoff at my attire. (I told him I was suffering from "beach withdrawal", a condition that occasionally afflicts land-locked Californians.) No, the tall person standing there wasn't Jeff, that fickle Indiana varmint; it was Chris. I believe that the winter just past was the one he spent at a fancy riding academy back east. Anyway, he'd promised to write to some outfits about another trail-guiding job for us. When he told me he had done so, I said, "Well?", and he said he thought we had a nibble. I asked where. He said, "Alaska".

I turned to him in shock, saying, "Are you crazy? Alaska, come on." Then the possibilities started to dawn. "Alaska......!" Wildlife I'd never seen, massive tracts of wilderness, practically the top of the planet. I was getting excited, but how were we going to get there? Chris tried to look nonchalant as he told me we would drive his Datsun pickup/camper up the Alaska Highway, of course—and by the way, we had to leave in 3 days!

We had been hired to pack horses through McKinley Park for the climbers. I believe it took us about a week of almost continuous driving to get there. Crossing through Idaho, I looked down into the low pasture we were passing and saw a cow chasing a coyote, shaking her horns at him as the coyote loped along, staying easily out of her reach. I remember the magnificent mountains around Hope, British Columbia, and some eerie mist along the road near Prince George. We saw Dall sheep with our binoculars at the Kluane Wildlife Refuge in the Yukon.

Then it was endless stretches of black spruce and muddy (unpaved!) road.

We made it to Mercer's, the guy that owned the only concession that ran horses in the park. 2 steps into his yard and I was attacked by his miniature Dachshund, who hung onto my pant leg even when I lifted him off the ground. I looked at Chris and said, "I hope this isn't a bad sign". The first pack trip was due to start in 2 days, and Mercer gave us little cabins to stay in. The first night at dinner—a delicious moose stew made by his wife—Mercer came right out and told me he didn't think I could do the job because I was a woman. Well! I was in good shape then, and was pretty offended by that remark. Talk about ruining the atmosphere of what was our first home-cooked meal in Alaska.

Chris and I talked it over. I told him I thought Mercer was a jerk and didn't particularly feel like busting my kiester for him, even though my pride wanted to prove him wrong. Chris agreed with my opinion of Mercer, but decided he'd go on one pack trip. But it was quite a commitment, because each pack trip lasted a month!

Chris said I could use his truck while he was gone, and after I told Mercer to "take this job and shove it"—although not in those exact words—Nikki and I cruised into the nearby town of Healy, population 70—mostly native—and went into the Healy Hotel to have some breakfast. The cafe inside had 16 seats, 12 at the counter and one table of 4. The bar was right next to it and was at least 3 times the size of the dining area. On the other side was the lobby with an ancient TV. Upstairs were the rooms. Both the town and hotel were built by the Alaska Railroad, for the Anchorage employees to lay over for the night, and the Fairbanks guys for a few hours in the day, as Healy was much closer to Fairbanks.

I got to talking to the friendly waitress and told her about Mercer and all, and she asked what I was going to do. I said I didn't know yet, but was thinking of driving down south a bit and checking out a few

dog racing kennels. She said I should think about working there, at the
Healy Hotel. I said no thanks, I'd just spent the winter in Colorado
waiting tables, and could use a bit of a break. Later on when she came
by to give me the check, she mentioned it again, saying they really
needed another waitress right now. I asked how much it paid, and she
said, "$450 a month and free room and board." My jaw dropped. This
was alot of money! We'd heard wages were high in Alaska, but wow.
Allrighty then—maybe I could do a little more waitressing.

I remember the manager, Elsie. She was one of those women that
had what I call the "bitch look" permanently etched on her face. Then
there was Earl, a really nice old guy that did some of the cooking. And
I haven't forgotten Virginia, that elderly spitfire that once dropped a
just-finished B.L.T. on the floor in the kitchen, told me to hush, picked
it up, put it on the plate, and ordered me to take it out to the customer.
When I returned, she asked me whose sandwich it was. When I told
her, she said, "Good, he's an asshole." I made my own sandwiches after
that.

I quickly got to know the railroad guys, as they came in every
day. At first they had me bamboozled into believing they were all
pilots. Ernie, one of the engineers, let me ride to Fairbanks in the
engine. I guess all the trains were pretty old. The way they were de-
signed inside, it was really hard to see out the windows in the front.
I was sitting on the left side one time, when Ernie shouted "Look!" I
jumped over to his side and there was a cow moose, running as fast as
we were going, which was about 40 miles an hour right then. It was
an awesome sight, this huge ungainly animal running like a horse,
with her neck stretched out and ears laid back. Then she started to
veer towards us, as if she wanted to cross the tracks in front of the
train. My heart went into my throat, imagining the horrible crash,
but Ernie coolly reached up and gave the horn a couple of toots, and
she straightened up on her course. He goosed the throttle and we
soon left her behind.

I pretty much could ride the train whenever I wanted, for free. But there were only the 2 routes—north and south. People that lived out in the bush could flag down the train anytime, anywhere. Ray, one of the conductors, told me that the moose sometimes traveled on the tracks in winter, when the snow was heavy, and that the wolves knew this, and sometimes took advantage of it.

One of the railroad workers in the yard at Fairbanks asked me if I wanted to drive one of the engines. I only hesitated for a second before excitement flooded through me and I said yes. We were in the yard itself, and didn't go very fast at all, but it's an incredible feeling to experience having control of this immense metal machine weighing many tons.

The weather in Healy, which is located in the interior of Alaska—between 2 mountain ranges—has pretty drastic extremes of temperature. It has gotten to 60 degrees below and more in the winter, and in the summer when I was there, it went as high as 90 for 3 days—the locals were freaking out. There were tons of mosquitos, which made it pretty miserable being outside. But occasionally there were these perfect days, sunny, not too hot, and just enough wind to keep the little bloodsuckers away.

It was a day like this that I was poking around between the railroad tracks (which were only 20 feet from the hotel's front door), and the Nenana River. Earl saw me going out the door and reminded me that there was a grizzly in the area—just what I didn't want to hear. I was down the slope exploring with Nikki among the lush green grasses and willows on the riverbank. I sat down in a sunny spot to enjoy the feel of the earth beneath me and the wonderful plant smells. Suddenly a tremendous thrashing noise, along with Nikki's savage barking, came from my left, towards the river. My whole body instantly turned to jelly. I thought of Earls' warning, and for a few seconds, I couldn't move. Then the ruckus stopped, and I stood up

Chris at one of the passes near Mt. McKinley

Chris throwing "sticks" for Tedward

on my wobbly knees. I waited, wondering if I could even run on my legs, and when the commotion started up again, I was just on the point of trying to sprint up the slope to the tracks and high-tail it for the hotel's front door. But when it became quiet again, I paused. I told myself that I had not heard any bear-like growling or roaring sounds, and if I didn't find out what had Nikki in such a dither, I'd curse myself forever for being a weenie. So I stealthily eased back toward the sound, holding still during the outbursts, and advancing during the calms. In about 2 minutes I could see through the dense leaves, and was pretty relieved by what I saw.

It was a youngish-looking (though still pretty enormous) female moose, innocently trying to browse on the willows when Nikki happened on her and began disturbing her digestion. Nikki didn't know I was there, so I got to watch her in action as she lurked and loitered around the edge of the glade until she got up her courage again to charge and lunge at the moose, who then would lay back her ears and charge right back, trampling everything in her path including some sizable saplings—thus the crashing noises. Nikki was always able to evade her hooves, luckily. I decided not to call attention to myself, in case the moose fancied something a bit slower-moving to chase, and after backing up a ways, turned and made my way up the railroad embankment. I then called to Nikki, but there was no way she was going to give up on that high level of entertainment.

I asked some of the native kids, who often hung around the hotel, to let me know when Nikki came back, as I had to start my shift. They were always up for any kind of outdoor adventure, and happily rushed off toward the river. About 20 minutes later, I heard their feet pounding on the wooden stairs to the back door of the kitchen, yelling, "Caryl, Caryl! Nikki's coming!" I stepped outside, and here she came, tongue hanging out a mile, bounding toward the hotel. I examined her all over, and found 2 spots, one on the right shoulder, and one on the right hip, that looked like they'd been shaved. It puzzled me for a minute, until I remembered someone telling me about the sharpness of moose hooves.

I never really appreciated kids until I went to Alaska. There was one native family with 5, ranging in ages 6 to 12. I remember Tony, 10, and Nick, 12. They were just such a blast, and not whiny, spoiled, tantrum-throwing little brats like you see so often in a so-called civilized town. They loved to explore, both their physical environment and with their minds, and they loved music. I roamed all over that area with those kids, who were granted a pretty amazing amount of freedom. The girl in that family, Carrie, around 9 years old, told me how she'd been chased by a bull moose during the rutting season. (I was coming to realize that every person in Alaska had either a bear or a moose story, and often both.) These kids were knowledgeable about the local wild animals and plants. They were excellent company.

There was a 15-year-old girl named Joy that used to ride the train from Anchorage to work as a maid in the hotel. I went with her to nearby Otter Lake sometimes, and we would borrow a canoe from 2 guys who had a cabin on the shore. These guys also had the biggest, hairiest husky-type dogs I'd ever seen; they made Nikki look tiny. The first time we took the canoe out, Nikki refused to get in, so we left her on the beach. As we paddled out into the lake, she started pacing back and forth and howling to the heavens. Finally she ran into the water and swam out to us. We hauled her on board, and were immediately grossed out. There was a good reason why no humans ever swam in that lake: it was infested with leeches. We had to start picking them off Nikki's fur the instant she was in the boat, otherwise some would fall off her fur and attach themselves to us.

The sunsets on the lake were incredible. And it wasn't just the colors, and that they were reflected in the water—it was the fact that the sun didn't set until around midnight, and it rose a few degrees and a couple of hours later in the northeast! Everyone in town had thick shades on their windows; otherwise it was hard to sleep. I remember often being awake at 1 a.m., watching the Fairbanks train roll in.

Ray, the conductor I mentioned, was a decent, conservative sort of guy, and Joy and I would sometimes play practical jokes on him. The only one I can actually remember is short-sheeting his bed. If we were awake when he was ready to turn in, we would stand at the bottom of the stairs, waiting for the cussing.

When Chris got back from the pack trip, he quit Mercer's outfit. He said Mercer was an insufferable pain in the ass, or something to that effect. Elsie hired him to cook on Virginia's days off, which meant he worked almost every day of the week. The railroad guys quickly dubbed him Mickey Mouse, as he was fond of wearing a certain Disney tank top. If I was the waitress when Chris was the cook, we had way too much fun. If I was giving him a hard time in the kitchen, when I went to take a plate out to the counter, he'd chuck something at me just as I got to the doorway. I got in the habit of hunching my shoulders in anticipation for the blow. This would cause Chris to emit that peculiar hee-hawing sound I can hear in my head to this day.

While Chris was gone, I often drove his pickup 5 miles down the road to the park entrance. I spent an hour or 2 most nights, hoping to see a wolf, but never did. I was lucky to have a close encounter with a porcupine that was walking toward me but apparently not watching where he was going. I stood still and he finally realized I was there when he was only about 3 feet away. He was in mid-step with one front paw lifted and he did an about face without setting that paw down. (I let him get that close because in those days I could move fast when I had to, unlike now.)

Chris, the lucky sod, saw a wolf on his pack trip, by the river early one morning. He said we should go backpacking on the same trail they took the climbers up, that the view from McGonagal Pass was amazing. It didn't take much arm-twisting. I asked one of the neighbors if he'd watch Nikki, and he agreed. We loaded up our packs and drove to the park, hopped on the park shuttle—an ancient school bus—and rode 4 hours on a dirt road to Wonder Lake. On that ride we saw fantastic scenery on a grand scale. We also saw 14 grizzlies.

Anybody that had the idea they could outrun a grizzly had their minds totally changed because of that bus ride. One sub-adult bear crossed right in front of our stopped bus and galloped swiftly up a steep hill on the other side, muscles rippling under his yellowish-brown fur. Then he turned and stood on his hind legs, sniffing the air in our direction. Everyone was glued to the windows, in awe. It was impressive, and I felt a shiver of fear in my gut. I had never camped out in grizzly country.

When we had gone to the park office to get our backcountry permit, the rangers gave us advice on bears and other things. Chris was asking about renting crampons and poles and ice axes; he was actually considering crossing the snout of Muldrow Glacier! As neither of us had any experience on ice, I firmly put the kibosh on that idea. So the rangers told us that crossing the McKinley River could be a bit tricky, that you could not see the bottom because of the "milkiness" of the water—due to debris from the glacier—but the good news was, there were no large rocks underneath, just fairly uniform pebbles. The McKinley was a "braided" river, and there would be many channels of varying sizes within it, as Chris already knew, having crossed it with the pack horses. We were instructed to look for the ripples closest together; that meant shallower water. They cautioned us that each of the larger channels would have a deeper section where the flowing water created a furrow. The bigger person, ideally holding a staff or large stick of some sort, should step into the channel first, facing the water, sidestepping, with the smaller person behind at an angle, holding onto their pack. The rangers also warned us that once we were in the water, we would not be able to hear each other because of the roar of the water.

It rained at least part of every day for the 9 days we were out. I remember the first section, before the river, was called Destruction Trail.

Aptly named. It was boggy and full of tree roots, and within 20 minutes my shoulders and back were objecting mightily to my ill-fitting pack. We stopped and Chris very gallantly took some of my load. His pack probably weighed over 70 pounds. I had to chuckle when I spotted a small glass bottle of One-A-Day vitamins sticking out of of one of the pockets.

My first sight of the swift-moving, dull grey river was not one to fill me with cheer. A look across the mile-wide river bar, with nary a tree in sight, meaning nothing to tie a rope to, was truly daunting. I expressed my doubts to Chris, who assured me it wouldn't look so bad after some macaroni and cheese and a good night's sleep. Right.

He set up the tiny 2-person tent and lit a mosquito coil inside, and closed the flap. Then we stood about 15 feet away, letting the mosquitos surround us. On Chris's signal, we sprinted for the tent, dived in, and quickly zipped the flap. Chris would then lay on his back, watching for stray mosquitos, and kill them one by one. This became a nightly ritual.

Another nightly ritual was the "scattering of the mothballs". I had read that bears (and other animals) hate the way they smell, so every evening I would dutifully surround our tent with the aromatic little spheres. I tried to forget the old sourdough I'd told my plans to, who chewed his mustache for a few seconds and drawled, "Yep, I shot a bear oncet—and he jes' reeked o' mothballs!"

The mosquitos down in the river bottoms were unbelievable. Their drone literally sounded like a small airplane flying somewhere nearby. There were stories about criminals being abandoned sans clothing on the tundra, who were drained of blood within days. Just the noise alone seemed capable of driving us nuts. Chris, as he did in Wyoming, took to spraying repellant directly on his face, but now it was Deep Woods Off, rather than Cutter's. I finally resorted to wearing a mosquito net, which cut down on visibility, but avoided that chemical sting.

We crossed a total of about 20 channels, including rivulets, the next morning without incident. Before stepping into the river, we followed yet another hint from the rangers and undid our bellybands, in case we should lose our footing and have to shuck off our packs in order to swim. After clearing the last channel, we were pretty stoked. But we were to be humbled on the way back.

I remember coming to Turtle Hill, labeled on our USGS topographic map, sometime after the river crossing. We rounded a curve in the trail and there was a good-sized hillock that had been torn up as if by a small bulldozer. There was a rank smell in the air. The hairs on my arms stood up as I noticed the obvious huge claw marks in the dirt: this was the site of a grizzly trying to rout out some ground squirrels, and not too long ago either. Chris didn't seem overly disturbed, but I could feel myself entering into a state of extreme alertness, driven by fear. It was if my neck became a few inches longer as I quickly scanned the area, watching for movements in the foliage, or perhaps a glimpse of brownish fur. The trail led right through the willow thicket, and Chris reminded me that we were supposed to shake our "bear bells"—making noise so as not to surprise anything large, toothy, and potentially cranky. As we moved forward, I bellowed out John Denver's "Country Boy", which we heard on the jukebox in the hotel several times a day. Chris, trying to be humorous, said, "You would have to pick that one." I suggested he try conjuring up his donkey laugh, which was a pretty safe bet to scare off anything that moved.*

The black spruce near the river were not very tall—maybe up to 8 feet at best. After the willow thickets on the far side of the river, we came into the open and realized we were above timberline—at only 2500 feet elevation. Turtle Hill was the first substantial uprising of the land. My bear fears were becoming a bit of an obsession, but I consoled myself with the thought that for the next week, we at least had a clearer view of the land around us. But there was one thing that bothered me: since we couldn't hang our food from a tree, nor bury it in the ground because of the permafrost, nor leave it outside because of the parka squirrels, we had to keep it in the tent at night. I remember standing at the crest of a ravine, sharing a salami with Chris. It figures that Mr. I'm-Not-Afraid-of-Grizzlies would bring along the smelliest of preserved meats. But to give him credit, he chucked it in the ravine after we ate as much as we could. And no, this was not close to where we camped for the night.

The tent was pale green, and alot of light came through, making it hard to sleep. I had another good reason for being awake most of every night: the noises outside. If I heard something close to the tent, I would instantly break into a sweat from head to toe. I never experienced anything like this before or since. It didn't help that we couldn't see out, so I was left to guess whether it was just the squirrels, a porcupine, a fox—or something much, much larger, creeping up on us slowly and stealthily. Chris would be noisily sawing logs next to me, and I'd be wishing hateful things on him, and cursing myself for not bringing some sort of sleeping aid. But wait—that wouldn't help, we needed to be awake to make a quick getaway! But if we did manage to get out of the tent, where would we go? These were the thoughts that ran through my head in continuous loops every night.

Using the latrine, to put it politely, was it's own kind of adventure, not only because of the possibility of ambush, but because of the mosquitos. If you didn't start spraying your keister the second you dropped trou, you risked getting at least 100 bites in the time it took you to take a whiz. Once while looking for a bit of privacy, I found an enormous moose antler. After I did my duty, I dragged it back to Chris and said, "Would you mind carrying this back for me?" Since it weighed about 40 pounds, he declined, and not too politely either. I guess chivalry only extends so far. By the 4th day I was so tired I could barely drag myself up the trail. I know there were 2 creeks before the pass, Clear Creek and Cache Creek. Both were pretty fast-moving, though only about knee-deep, as opposed to the river, which had been up to the tops of my thighs. Since I was developing a blister, Chris offered to ferry me and then my pack across. I can't remember if it was before or after the pass that Chris, after he'd hoisted me on his back, caught his boot toe on a root and down we crashed into the ice cold water, causing alot of curses, insults, and laughter. That provided a needed bit of comic relief.

The pass itself was magnificent. I remember toiling up the rocky final approach, and seeing a rough cross made of broken ski poles along the side—one of a previous winter's victims—a reminder that though it was now summer, we were in some of the roughest, most challenging terrain on earth. When we stepped out to where we could see the actual pass itself, it was mind-blowing. There were 2 huge glaciers converging, and the whole landscape was a stark but sublime combination of black, white, and blue. The accumulated soil, blown by the wind, formed black patterns on the tops of the glaciers. You could see down into a few crevasses, some showing shades of turquoise and aquamarine inside that brought the Caribbean to mind. The sky was intense blue for a change, with puffy white clouds and not a raindrop in sight. And to increase the wonder of it all, a lone golden eagle soared over the glacier nearest to us. And last but not least, Mt. McKinley was visible all the way to its summit. That was only 1 of 2 times I saw the whole mountain that summer. Blisters, rain, bear fears, mosquitos, sore muscles, lack of sleep—it was all worth it to see this beautiful sight.

I'm pretty sure we were at the pass on the 6th day, meaning it only took us 3 days to get back to the trailhead at Wonder Lake. The only thing I remember from the trip back, other than the rain, was one single caribou bull, framed against a background of red and gold brush, with the snowy peaks behind. We'd been hoping to see a whole herd, and the rangers thought we might, as they told us there were many caribou passing through the park around the time we started out, but we only saw the one.

The roar of the river as we approached was much louder than it was before; even Chris, always wanting to downplay any possible risks, admitted it. It was mid-day when we got to the river bar, and we proceeded to load the bottoms of our packs with rocks as ballast—since we'd been eating our toted-in food every day and had lightened our load quite a bit. One thing I did differently: I attached a piece of rope to the top and bottom of Chris's pack, so it ran down the middle, giving me something easier to hang onto than the packframe, which was awkward to reach around to. As soon as we sidestepped down into the first of the large channels, I knew we were in for a battle, because the water was noticeably colder than our first time across.

We got through about 4 of the big ones with no mishaps. It's a strange feeling, being alone out there in the middle of the rushing river, or standing on the gravel bar, with absolutely no sign of man, no helicopters, no horses, no 4-wheel-drive vehicles, no help to be had if you got into trouble. Just 2 puny little humans, surrounded by water, with the wide sky overhead, alone. We were hip-deep in the 5th channel, sidestepping in sync, when my feet were suddenly swept out from under me and I was instantly stretched out full-length by the current, still holding on to the rope with my left hand. The water was surging just under my right eye, and my body began to twist to the right from the weight of the heavy pack pulling my shoulders around. I could see and feel that Chris was struggling with everything he had to keep his feet, but all I could look at was the water. I had no thoughts in my head, it was weird. I somehow decided not to let my pack go. I couldn't shout, even if I thought Chris could hear me, as my mouth was under the water. It seemed like either a few seconds or an eternity that we were locked in the struggle against the river. Then, I have no idea how, I was able to get my feet back under me and without any overt signal, we both began working our way out of the channel, back the way we'd come into it.

When we got onto the gravel bar and took off our packs, I remember Chris staying silent, pacing up and back, allowing me time to regroup. I crouched and hugged my knees, soaked to the skin all over and shivering in the cool air. I didn't feel afraid when I was in the water, but as soon as I got up out of it and onto the land, fear came over me like a cocoon. The only thing to be done was to face it: as much as I didn't want to even look at, let alone get into the water again, it was the only way out.

After about 10 minutes, Chris said one word: "Ready?" I nodded, got up, and we studied the channel and chose a different place to cross. We made it. I felt in my bones that we would succeed in crossing the rest of the channels, and I was right.

I was pretty sure Chris felt the same way, although we didn't talk about it until the next day. When we stepped out of the final channel, Chris surprised me by hurling his staff into the water with an angry look on his face. I realized that he took it as a personal affront that the river had tested us in that way. I didn't share that feeling; I thought of it as damn lucky that we'd made it. If I had let go of the rope and been carried downstream, I would have had to jettison my pack and swim to the bank. But the problem was, I would never have been able to get back to where Chris was, because I needed his weight to ford the channels, and without it I would've had to swim, and each time would be carried farther down the river. This meant that Chris would have to leave his pack and float/swim down to where I was. But we wouldn't have the packs for added weight, and probably not the staff either. And how would we retrieve the packs? The gravel bars are not continuous, they break and merge, so it's not like you can walk down one for any distance. We'd have to recross some channels. Meanwhile, the temperature would be dropping, the rain again threatening, we'd have no dry gear, and we would miss the last shuttle bus back to the park entrance. Hypothermia would be stalking us.

We came out of the river in a different place than we went into it 9 days before; I believe we were a bit to the east. To get up to the road by the shortest route we had to push our way through a dense thicket of bushes. This wasn't easy, at least for me, being soaked, exhausted, and so relieved to be on dry land it made my head swim and my body feel even weaker. The silver lining was, many of the bushes were loaded with blueberries—the best on earth. We stuffed handfuls of them in our mouths with every step, while keeping a sharp eye out for the bears, because they loved them too. Those Toklat grizzlies may be scary, but at least they have good taste.

I vaguely remember Chris carrying me piggy-back up the last rise. I think one of my knees was bothering me. Finally there was the road just ahead—and we could hear the sound of an old engine with not much muffler left—the bus!—heading away from us, back toward the ranger station. Don't ask me how he had the energy, but Chris ran down the road after it, shouting and waving. I always knew he was tougher than a boiled owl, but this trip proved it beyond any doubt. Thankfully the driver stopped, and we boarded.

By the time the 4-hour trip was over and we were back at the entrance station, I was nearly incoherent with cold. I have no memory of getting off the bus and into Chris's truck, or of arriving in Healy, but I knew I had to see Nikki before I went to the hotel. I remember her racing up and down next to the railroad tracks, ecstatic that we were back. One of the guys in town said hi and I couldn't even answer. I think a sound came out of my mouth, but I'm not sure. He said, "Are you allright?" I nodded and started toward the hotel door, hoping I could stay on my feet. I made it inside and up the stairs and to the shower, and with the hot water pouring down on me, I began to come back to myself. After that I went right to the kitchen and made myself a huge roast beef sandwich, and wolfed it down, sharing some with Nikki right there in the cafe, since Elsie wasn't around. I have no idea what Chris was doing right then. I only had the strength to focus on warmth, food, and rest.

When we talked the next day, we agreed that that was the most awesome and hairy backpacking trip either of us had ever taken. Chris asked me how far up the water was on me just before I lost my footing. I tapped my hip bone (in those days I could actually locate my hip bones) and said, "Right here." He said, "Wow." He told me that when he finally was able to get a look behind him, and saw me down in the water, he said all of his will almost left him. He asked if I was scared, and I told him I didn't feel it until I got up on the bar, and that when I was in the water, it was as if I didn't have the usual thought processes—no Howard Cosell in my head, commenting on everything. I asked him what my face looked like, if it showed terror, shock, or what. He thought for a minute and said, "You looked...businesslike."**

A few days later, when we were again discussing our shared adventure, Chris asked me whether I would have gone with him if I knew ahead of time what the trip would be like. I didn't have to ponder very long:

"No".

Chris had a one-word comment:

"Weenie".

Tedward, the athlete

Tedward and Caryl ready to leave for their southwest trip, 1978

Chapter 17

The rest of the summer seemed to fly by. I worked a little longer in the hotel, maybe just 2 or 3 weeks. Chris got a job with the Alaska Railroad, and when he was on a break in Fairbanks one day, he walked a ways into the forest and surprised a wolverine. Was I jealous? Yes indeed.

You could feel the air getting colder by mid-August. Chris and I said goodbye for the time being, as he wanted to keep his new job for awhile, and I wanted to head south toward California, see my family and then travel back to Colorado and Joe. Chris uttered his favorite farewell phrase, "Stay on top." Nikki and I boarded the train to Anchorage, where I spent a few days with Ray and his housekeeper and her daughter. This little girl loved Nikki. I remember seeing the movie Towering Inferno while I was there, and going to a bar called Chilkoot Charlie's, where someone had been shot the week before. An old boozer wanted me to dance with him and after refusing politely twice, I had to get a little ornery to get him to back off. That set Ray to chuckling. I scowled at him and said, "What, you expect me to dance with that guy?" and he said, "No, I just got a kick out of the shocked look on his face when you cussed."

The 4 of us rode the train to Whittier one day, and lo and behold, it was sunny—definitely not the norm, I was told. I remember the steep mountains falling right into the water, making me think of the fjords of Norway. Then there were the houses on stilts, which was puzzling until Ray told me that the coastal areas can get up to 80 feet of snow in the winter!

Nikki and I flew to Juneau soon after, and were treated to yet another gorgeous setting, with high mountains sporting artistically-placed snowbanks, and the water at the beginning of the Inside Passage reflecting them. We boarded the ferry Columbia, and began a 3-day journey to Seattle. I remember it cost $70, if you didn't mind throwing your sleeping bag down in the solarium, a large, covered open-air space on the deck. Nikki had to stay in her crate in the hold, where I went several times a day to walk her in the little sawdust-covered dog yard they had set up.

The solarium was a blast, crowded with backpackers and their gear, and lots of happy young people who had just spent some quality time in Alaska. One guy had a huge, intact set of caribou antlers tied above his sleeping bag. Every inch of space appeared to be taken, but I finally found an 18-inch opening in one row. It was great to relax and trade stories with people, and enjoy the smooth ride, sunshine, and the ever-changing view of water and mountains and islands.

With what Chris called "typical girl logic", I figured since I wasn't paying for a stateroom, I'd eat in the restaurant for dinner. I think it was our last night that we entered Queen Charlotte Sound, and there went our smooth ride. The ship started to pitch and roll in a very lively manner, causing many of the diners to leave their tables rather suddenly and make for the exit. I girded my loins and was determined to eat a small but complete meal. By the time I was finished, the dinner crowd was reduced to me and one table of 4. Now the only problem was walking out of there without falling on my face. I managed to stagger crazily to the door, and the route from there to the solarium had plenty of handrails. The camping crowd was in a cheerful uproar, although I did notice a few unfortunate souls making offerings over the rail. The fog held the ship in a close embrace as we rode out the swells. Within an hour, we got into the lee of some more islands, the fog dissipated and everything calmed down. But we had another surprise in store for us that night.

Most of the young people on board, especially those who had spent the summer engaging in various sports such as hiking, backpacking, glacier and high mountain skiing, rafting, etc., were feeling mighty restless on that last night of the trip down the Inside Passage. The talking and laughing were still going strong at midnight, as I was relaxing on top of my down bag, enjoying the cool night air. Then someone said the words, "Northern lights", and there was an instantaneous reaction. It seemed that everyone under the solarium's cover jumped up in a body and ran out to the open part of the deck. Low in the northwest part of the sky was a large area of the night sky covered with green, undulating curtains of light.

For many of us, it was our first time seeing the Aurora Borealis. It was so beautiful and other-worldly, nobody could look away. It was there for at least 40 minutes, when I finally went back to my spot. I don't remember it changing size or color during that time, but it was constantly in motion. It was interesting listening to others talk about auroras they'd seen that were very different. We were only a few hours north of Seattle at that point, and it was the middle of August, so I felt pretty lucky to have seen it.

Jeff, our old trail-guiding buddy, had somehow found his way to Washington and met me at the dock in Seattle. I only remember one thing: stopping at a fruit stand where I bought $10 worth of plums, nectarines and peaches, which was alot in those days. I hadn't had fruit all summer, and I didn't show much restraint as I gobbled it all up within the next hour. I waited for my colon to retaliate, but miraculously there were no untoward effects. (I wouldn't try it in these modern times though; "Colleen" has become quite the little tyrant.)

I flew Nikki to Colorado, caught the Greyhound and headed to Santa Monica, visited family, and then it was back to the Rockies, Estes Park, and Joe.

Chapter 18

Now we're coming up on Tedward Time. If I remember right, the Oldhams stayed into December that year, and until then I crashed at Flossie's house, one of a group of little cabins on a hill not far from the county landfill. We called the place "Dump View Estates". I think she and Jeff were starting to make eyes at each other around that time. After I moved back into the Oldhams, I remember Jeff and I sitting in the old wooden rockers in front of the fire one evening. I felt totally comfortable with Jeff as a friend by then, and I told him why I had left Jackson Hole so suddenly 2 years before. He was amazed. (Typical man, no idea what's going on). I asked him whatever happened with his girlfriend from Cody. He said she never showed up!

There was a guy named Kevin with a red VW convertible named Scarlet. He was kind of an odd character; I forget how I met him. But it was sometime that winter that he first brought Sue, who later became and still is one of my best friends, up to Estes. I remember riding in the back seat in Scarlet, yelling "Hyah, hyah!" when going uphill on icy roads with the top down. He also had a VW bus, and he and Sue and I were in it when Kevin had a meltdown one day over the tape-deck not working right, screaming with rage and throwing the loops of tape all over, with Sue and I looking at each other, astonished. Now you may think I'm painting a rather unfavorable picture of this person, and you would be right. There's a good reason for it, which I'll get to in a minute.

Sue, who was Kevin's girlfriend then, used to like tormenting him as much as I did. One day when they were both at the cabin and had just finished eating, Sue and I took the plates and put them on the floor for Nikki and Bean, her husky mix. Kevin thought that was gross, but he'd seen us do it before. However when I picked up the plates and started putting them back in the cupboard, he couldn't keep quiet. Sue and I tried to tell him that a dog's mouths had fewer germs than a human's but he was outraged. We assured him that this was standard procedure for many dog owners. He couldn't get it that we were messing with him. He was really afraid that all this time we'd been feeding him off of plates that hadn't been washed with soap and water. His face was getting flushed and we thought he might stroke out on us, so we finally relented and told him it was all a joke. Did he think it was funny? He did not. He stomped out of the cabin and went for a walk. When he came back about a half hour later, we all pretended that everything was normal.

Kevin also thought some of the things we ate were weird, like Bisquick coffee cake with double the streusel topping mix, white cake with white frosting, and most of all, Pillsbury vanilla frosting straight out of the can. Obviously Kevin had no sweet tooth. When we discovered how delicious that frosting tasted by itself, Sue and I would often buy it just for its own sake, keeping it on hand in the 'fridge and bringing it out to pass it around when people came over, especially if there had been any weed-smoking going on. Picture it—people taking a swipe with a finger and then giving it to the next person to do the same. Kevin would roll his eyes and tell us how disgusting we were. I wanted to hold him on the floor and stuff some in his mouth, but Sue said no, remember the tape deck—he might become homicidal.

I do remember one good experience I had with Kevin. He and I were in Scarlet driving on the loop in Rocky Mountain National Park that goes through Horseshoe Park and up and over to the other entrance. We stopped on the flat near the elbow bends of Fall River, and walked out toward the water. It was autumn, and the clouds were hanging low, obscuring the large peaks surrounding the valley. We each were standing on our own bend of the river, about 50 yards apart, and

I was appreciating the stillness, looking around at the landscape and the unusual clouds, when a single coyote began to howl. It was a pure-toned, mournful sound, yet somehow with a bit of lightheartedness to it. Kevin and I looked at each other, not saying anything. I believe he felt the magic of that moment also.

Horseshoe Park was also the best place to watch the elk during the rut, or mating season. The bulls with their magnificent antlers would gather their harems of cows, expending alot of energy trying to keep them together and prevent other bulls from stealing them. You didn't have to leave your car, you could see exciting shoving matches and hear antlers clacking together from only a little distance. But the best thing was the bugling. The noise that comes out of these large, macho animals is unbelievable. They throw their heads back, open their mouths and emit a sound that starts down low, swoops up the scale to climax in a piercing, valley-filling high note, sometimes with overtones. Then it rattles quickly back down, sometimes ending in a few grunts. "Bugling" describes it pretty well.

Kevin, that rascal, had a certain propensity for, shall we say, illegal endeavors. For example, it was amazing how neatly a large bale of alfalfa, Joe's favorite type of hay, fit into Scarlet's back seat. But he crossed the line when he decided to liberate my cross-country skis from the third cabin on the Oldham's property that was used for storage. He did the dirty deed outside of ski season, or obviously I would have noticed right away. He picked his time perfectly. I have no concrete proof it was him; let's just say I had a knowing in my bones.

Chapter 19

That winter of 1975-76 I had some knee problems, and waitressing wasn't possible. As I mentioned, Paula at the bookstore hired me for some odd jobs, such as painting. Winter became a sore trial for me as I couldn't get out to enjoy it. But alot of friends from the past year were still around, like Beth and Karen, Kathy and Flossie, and others. I remember Karen rolling up in her giant '57 station wagon she called "The Green Machine". That thing had more room inside than most apartments I've lived in. The tires were bald, and how she got up the hill to the Oldham's was a mystery. But she was a regular and welcome guest as we played guitars and drank tea many times during the cold season.

Sometimes we'd have people over and Joe would be hanging around and someone would ask if they could ride him around the yard. Usually these were the young guys we knew, always eager to show off for any ladies present. But gentle old Joe had a few tricks up his sleeve for these cowboy wannabes. He would be a perfect gentleman if there was a child on his back; I didn't even have to have a halter or a rope on him, he would walk along beside me like a dog, the kid holding on to his mane, thrilled. But put a guy or gal in their teens or twenties on him, and he became a devil. At first he would refuse to go, until they kicked him one time too many, then he would take off like a rocket, swing a sharp curve at the end of the gravel driveway, and gallop swiftly back, coming to a screeching halt by the porch. If whoever was on board survived this, they usually didn't ask to ride him again.

Joe had a special treat for Beth one day. She wanted to try him out, and as soon as she got on his back, I could tell by the look on his face that she was in for it. He stood stock still, ignoring her kicks, until finally I got a short rope and popped it near him. He took off suddenly, doing his most bone-jarring trot, so that by the time they reached the gate at the end of the driveway, Beth was bent forward with her arms clutching his neck. She almost slid off, but rallied, regained her balance and was able to sit upright again as Joe gunned it and thundered back toward the cabin. But instead of aiming for his usual place, he veered a little and headed for 2 young ponderosa pines that were only about 4 feet apart. I saw Beth stiffen up, and a second later she was on the ground, falling right on the rocks in front of the trees.

As soon as I saw she wasn't hurt, I burst out laughing. Her face was like chalk as I helped her up and dusted her off. "God Caryl, why didn't you tell me he was such a maniac!", she said, semi-pissed. "Did he do that on purpose?" I managed to croak out "Yes", amidst my breathless cackling. Joe ambled over to his favorite rose bush and began plucking off rose hips. I thought he wore an especially contented look on his face; if he was a human I would have high-fived him. Not that I was using him to get even or anything, for Beth always showing me up on skis.

The Oldham's porch that became one of Joe's favorite hangouts was the scene of a remarkable moment with a hummingbird. It was getting to be spring—and Tedward Time—and Sue and I came out the screen door and crossed the porch, with me in front, when I saw a hummingbird right there at the feeder that hung from the young ponderosa. We both stopped, and the hummer lifted off the feeder, turned toward me, and hovered there, really close. Without thinking about it I reached up slowly and caressed its chest and belly with the back of one finger. I did this a few times, and he didn't fly away until a few seconds after I'd pulled my hand away. I turned to look at Sue and we both were in awe. I actually felt his heart beating. I've since heard that hummingbirds are among the most fearless of birds, because they can fly so quickly in any direction, including backwards.

So we have now caught up with ourselves, and Tedward has made his journey from the plains to the mountains, about to embark on a life of amazing adventures, such as few dogs ever experience. We will pick up his story in late July,1976, just after our 4-night trip to Meadow Mountain, where Nikki encountered the porcupine.

Chapter 20

I worked at Wild Basin Livery in Rocky Mountain National Park, near the town of Allenspark, about 20 miles south of Estes, for a few weeks in July and August of 1976. It was my 3rd job as a trail guide and wrangler. The scenery was outstanding, as it was all over most of the front range. The Wild Basin drainage leading down from the mountains was alot narrower than that of Moraine Park, so you didn't get the same type of grand sweeping views. Chris may correct me on this, but I believe either the glacier that carved out the Wild Basin area was alot smaller than the one that formed Moraine Park, or this particular valley was not formed by a glacier.

Tedward was about 7 months old, and he got his first taste of being tied up during the times I was taking rides out, as it was national park land and dogs were not allowed on the trails. He did get a chance to exercise his lungs at these times, much to the annoyance of our boss, Don. Don, like Dave at Grouse Creek, was not really a dog person. Come to think of it, Don wasn't much of a people person either. He was, if possible, even more fanatic than Steve, our Moraine Park manager, about the rides going out on time. I had a great lead horse that I used alternately with Joe; he was a big, tall Thoroughbred/Quarter horse cross named Ford. I had him saddled and waiting as the other wranglers, Chris—this one a girl—and Jenny, our alleged manager, and I helped the guests on their horses. There happened to be a lull in the general conversation as I put my boot in the high-up stirrup and lunged to mount. A loud ripping sound issued from my Sedgefields, as even though I was slim in those days, there was only so much wear and tear denim could take. We all laughed, and I eased myself down to sprint for the bunkhouse to change. But then I caught sight of Don, around the side of the barn out of sight of the guests, frowning and waving his arm frantically for me to get on and get going. Wow. Like the weenie I was, I did as he wished. My leg was like raw meat after that ride.

Our female wrangler Chris was 19, and a very nice person, but also a bit naive. Jenny was my age—23—and one of the most conniving, manipulative little bitches I ever had the misfortune to know. She would do anything to make herself look good in Don's eyes, and us look bad. One day I was so mad at something she'd done—I wish I could remember what—that I spent an entire 4-hour ride fuming, and was really going to give it to her when I got back. When I led my riders into the barn area, the last I saw of Jenny was her booted heels as she hustled around the side of the tack room. I believe she knew I'd reached my limit, at least for that day.

Our 4-hour trail up to Sandbeach Lake was extremely steep for the first half-mile or so. The park workers had imbedded 5-foot logs horizontally every few yards to form large steps up the first switchbacks to keep the soil from continually sliding. Our ponies and smaller horses used to rear on their hind legs to get their front feet high enough to get up onto the next level. Having the saddles cinched tight was essential; same with giving the riders a heads up to lean forward and grab the horn. After we got to where the incline was less severe, I used to stop my ride, dismount and check all the cinches, to make sure none had been loosened by the extreme flexing of the horses' bodies.

Sandbeach Lake was around 10,000 feet, and very scenic in that typical, high-altitude sort of way, with trees here and there—timberline being around 10,500'—snow banks tucked among the sharp peaks, vivid blue water and sky with puffy white clouds. But the trail itself was kind of boring, as you were pretty much enclosed by lodgepole pines the whole way, with not too many views. So after the challenging beginning, there was a long sleepy spell which made the stunning lake view especially welcome.

One day I was riding Ford, with 4 riders behind me, and we were going up the steps at the beginning, and I was turned in my saddle talking to the people. I didn't bother to look around as Ford took the first step, as his legs were so long he never had trouble negotiating any of them. I heard a dull "ping", but figured it was his just one of his iron horseshoes hitting a small rock, and continued my conversation. Suddenly I felt a strange sliding sensation. I whipped around, and the saddle was halfway off Ford's back—the cinch had broken! First reaction: reach for the mane. Oops—no mane—it had been "roached". (Clipped totally off.) Ford was just getting his back legs up onto the next level when I knew I had to jump, and did, but I couldn't quite keep my feet and fell back onto my kiester, still holding one rein. There was no room to spare right there, with a good-sized drop off to my right, and a steep bank up to the left, and Ford was snorting and looking like he wanted to run right over the top of me to get away from the saddle which was now on the ground and brushing his back legs, spooking him. I talked to him in a soothing voice, saying, "Ho, easy boy, you're ok", etc., and he was flicking his ears and shifting his legs but he didn't bolt. I was able to get up and move the saddle away and then give him some reassuring pats, while my guests expressed amazement at what had just happened, the whole thing probably taking only a minute or even less. I was very pleased with Ford for keeping his cool, because alot of horses wouldn't have been able to do so in that situation. Since we weren't all that far from the barn, I asked my riders to wait and I managed to get on Ford, who was a little over 16 hands, by climbing up the next step and then onto his back, and I rode back to the barn to get another saddle. Don just about had a fit. He yelled at me to get back to my riders, and he came hustling up the trail on his horse, carrying a saddle, and hurriedly put it on Ford himself. Did he ask if I was allright? He did not. He was pissed, and I knew it wasn't because I'd left my riders alone on the trail—it was because the ride was going to be late!

There were some good things about Wild Basin, and one of them was the way the golden-mantled ground squirrels would come up onto our legs when we were sitting on the shoeing platform, eating our sack lunches. After the first few days they would even eat a corn chip while sitting on you. They are cute little varmints, chubby with striped flanks, and looking somewhat like chipmunks on steroids, although with no stripes on the head. Every few days I couldn't resist grabbing one, just to feel their furry little bodies in my hand for a second. I did get bitten a few times, which I figured was only fair. I was glad Jenny didn't sit with us, because she hated all rodents. She took way too much pleasure in killing the dusky-footed wood rats (also known as pack rats) that would sometimes get into the tackroom.

On one of our first half-days off, Chris and I rode up the Pear Lake trail by ourselves, to see how far up we could get. There had been alot of snow that winter, and we hadn't opened this trail yet for rides. Pear Lake itself was somewhere around 10,200 feet, and we were about 2 miles below it when we came to a place where there was a large, sharp-edged angular rock jutting out right in the middle of the trail. It wouldn't have been much trouble for a hiker, but for a horse with slippery iron shoes, it didn't look too good. To the right was an almost perpendicular 10-foot bank rising up, and to the left, the trail dropped off about 8 inches to a muddy area with standing water all over it. I let Joe have his head to see what he wanted to do. I figured he'd go for the mud, as that looked better than trying to get over the rock, the only other option. Joe put his head down, sniffed at the rock, then turned to the left and lifted both his front feet almost together and plopped them down into the mud, and promptly sank past his fetlocks. I heard Chris behind me go, "Gawd".

Joe stood poised there for a few seconds, perhaps wishing for a do-over, then dropped his hind feet down, sinking all the way to his hocks. I felt like I was on the dentist's chair, being leaned back for a root canal. Chris, a woman of few words, said, "Gawwwwd!" There was a moment of tense expectancy, and I thought of trying to vault off Joe's back toward the trail. But Joe took action before I did, heaving and lungeing like a crazy thing, with me hanging on to the saddle horn like a dude. In the blink of an eye we were back on the trail, past the rock, both of us breathing heavily, with me still in the saddle. Chris's comment? The same, only louder: "GAWD!!" She dismounted, climbed over the rock herself, and her horse followed. Too bad I didn't think of that.

Every night we had dinner at the boss's house, which was down the dirt road and across and down the highway about a mile. One evening in late July, I was watching storm clouds move in from a window that faced east, while Don's wife was putting dinner on the table. Most of our storms came from the west; I wondered if this would be a bad one. As we sat down to eat, it began to rain, and before we finished our salads, it was so loud we could hardly converse. The thunder and lightning was intense. There was a loud pop, and the tv went off, and the rest of the power went a few minutes later. We finished up and Chris and Jenny and I opened the front door to look, and the water was ankle-deep between us and our pickup. We decided to wait for a lull, but it never came. Finally we dashed out, leaped in the truck, and as Jenny was starting the engine, a huge bolt hit the ground in the pasture not far in front of us. We made it out the driveway and onto the highway, and the downpour was way more than the windshield wipers could handle. We crept along and turned off toward the stables, the dirt road looking like a brown river coming down the hill. The old truck slid around quite a bit, but we made it to the bunkhouse, where Tedward, who was normally not bothered too much by thunder, looked especially happy to see us. Chris and I put our slickers on and went to check on the horses. Fortunately none of the them were touching the barbed wire fence. They were all standing hunched and with heads lowered, facing away from the wind, stoically enduring the drenching rain. We sloshed back to the bunkhouse and sat around or lay on our bunks in the dark, thinking that surely the storm would be over soon.

At 3:00 a.m. it was still booming and cracking, but the rain had mostly stopped. We could still see the flashes up around Mt. Alice. I found out later that 3 climbers I knew were up there, trapped above timberline during part of that storm. The other thing we didn't know was that there was a huge flood in the Big Thompson Canyon, which led from Estes Park to Loveland. It had rained 10 inches in an hour; the storm system had stalled right over our part of the Rockies. Many bodies had already been found, and there were over 100 missing. The sheriff's department told Don that there had been a 19-foot wall of water surging down the lower part of the canyon.

The total number of people that died turned out to be 182, if I remember right. The road and most of the houses and cabins along that highway were totally destroyed. Today there are signs along the rebuilt highway that say, "Climb to safety".

The trails were pretty wrecked, with mudslides and downed trees and branches scattered all over. The park service guys and a few of us wranglers—notably not Jenny—worked for 2 days to clear things up, and we opened for rides again the 3rd day after the storm. The freakiest story I heard was that of the climbers I mentioned. One of them, Harry, told us the story that they got caught on a big rock slab at around 12,000 feet, and the 3 of them separated and found shallow depressions where they could crouch on the balls of their feet—standard safety protocol for high-altitude thunderstorms. They would periodically have to stand up to keep their legs from cramping. It was one time when their buddy John did this, that the other 2 saw a bolt hit the rock about 20 feet from him, and a second later, travel upward through his body, making his skeleton glow orange through his skin. When we loudly expressed doubt at this, Harry swore up and down that he was telling the gospel truth. John was knocked unconscious, and didn't seem to be breathing—they thought he was dead. He came to after a few minutes of CPR, and was allright, though dazed and shaken. The only evidence it had happened was the metal of his pants zipper was totally fused. John, well-known as a "ladies' man" in town, said later that he thought maybe the powers that be were trying to tell him something.

With knee and back problems plaguing me, and knowing that Tedward wasn't having the greatest of times, I quit Wild Basin and took my animals back up to Estes Park and the Oldhams. Mr. and Mrs. Oldham were still there, (they usually left for their winter home in Ohio in the fall) but we were invited to stay in one of the guest cabins for as long as we wanted, rent free. Mrs. O. and I had a great time playing cards and talking about everything under the sun. Mr. O. was not an animal lover, but grudgingly bent to his wife's wishes and welcomed us and treated us well. I'm pretty sure that during this late summer of 1976 was the last time we stayed at that wonderful place.

Our one picture of some of the Grouse Creek Livery gang. That's Dave on the left, Brick sitting down, and my friend from the Marine Mammal Center, Holly on the right, who was visiting us.

Tedward, Caryl and Joe having a 3-way conversation at Stevenson's ranch, 1980

Chapter 21

So we are overlapping ourselves here in Tedward Time, and already having talked about our little adventures in 1977, '78, and part of '79, we will now continue with our second summer at Grouse Creek. It's not easy to remember what things happened in which summer. Chris (the guy Chris, not Chris the girl from Wild Basin) didn't actually work at Grouse Creek until the latter part of the second summer in 1979. Since I had introduced him to Claire, (who worked both summers), I take credit for the fact that they not only got married but are still married as of this writing. (Claire obviously has not only the tenacity of a terrier, but the tolerance of Buddha.) And let's not forget my other, equally awesome matchmaking feat: Jeff of Moraine Park fame, and Flossie, my friend and co-worker from Estes Park, were introduced to each other by me, got hitched, and are still together, having raised a passel of kids and grandkids in Montana.*

Back to Grouse Creek: there was a line shack up on top of Meadow Mountain that was used by sheepherders and others. On off-day rides if you got caught by a squall, it was a good place to hole up, with a large overhang to the porch to shelter your horse. I asked Dave what was beyond it, and he said there was a trail that went up over the ridge and down the next drainage. He said almost nobody went there and the trail might not even be passable. So of course we had to check it out.

I remember it being pretty windy the day that Joe and Tedward and I headed up the trail to see what we could see. Long past the line shack, in a heavily treed swale, we passed a group of hunters camped, and it kind of gave me the willies. Lots of men with guns and probably booze, and here's little old me with my horsie and my doggie. (And no weapons). But nothing happened and we continued on up the trail. As I dismounted so we could get up the last steep section more easily before dropping over the other side of the ridge, there was a huge boom, and my heart jumped—I'm pretty sure it was a shotgun, coming from the camp down below. We were struggling forward into the wind which was so strong right there that even Joe was being pushed around. The thought crossed my mind that we would be an easy target, out in the open on that steep slope, with no cover to get to fast. There was nothing to do but keep going, and about 10 minutes later, we topped out and started on the barely discernible trail down.

It was so steep that Joe was sliding on his back legs like you see in the old westerns. As we rapidly descended, I was really hoping we wouldn't have to retrace our steps. There were some small lakes among the trees, and the trail veered off to the right and entered the dense lodgepoles. And here we come to the aforementioned mudholes, that Joe luckily handled so well. Tedward had no trouble, tripping lightly around the very edges, or dropping down into the stream, or winding his way up higher through the trees. But Joe and I had to slog through every one, and it wasn't like liquid with a firm base, it was thick, black and sticky with no apparent bottom, judging by the way Joe flailed and struggled to get through. Each one was between 4 and 10 feet long, and covering the entire trail from side to side.

There were faded and tattered orange plastic flags attached to tree branches over most of the mudholes, so sometime in the last couple of years, a Forest Service crew had marked them to warn hikers and riders, and maybe skiers, for when the snow started to get slushy in the spring. Every time I saw either a flag or the big dark area ahead in the shadows, my stomach reacted. We forged on, Joe battling gamely, me in a constant state of anxiety. Then we saw the bear shit.

It was on a dry section, and I got off to inspect it, and you could see tons of berry seeds in it. I'm no expert on bear sign, but it looked pretty darn fresh. Joe sniffed it and blew out his breath as if disgusted, but didn't look overly alarmed. I called Tedward over and he took his turn to check it out, and I told them both that the main thing to remember was, that if we saw a bear, not to panic and lose our minds. Joe, that means no rearing and dumping me off, especially not in the mud. Tedward, that means no trying to fight the bear, but if you could get him to chase you in another direction besides towards us, that could be good. Just don't let him catch you.

In the next half-hour, we went through 3 more mudholes and saw 2 more shitpiles. I wanted to walk for awhile to give my kiester and Joe's back a rest, but I didn't dare—if we did see a bear and Joe took off, I'd stand a much better chance of staying with him if I was on his back. The stillness was getting to me, no birdsong, no wind down in the narrow valley, just the gurgle of the creek water and the thud of Joe's hooves. Then here it came: the sound of cracking branches to our left. Joe pricked his ears, my stomach clenched and I started to sweat. This is it, I thought, as the sound came closer. Then boom—a deer leapt the creek and then the trail—right in front of us, with guess-who chasing him. I don't remember what I did, but Joe jumped a little and kept on walking, hardly batting an eye. As the deer ran diagonally up the right-hand bank, I bellowed at Tedward. He didn't look the least bit guilty for scaring the crap out of me. He looked happy and proud of himself, as if to say see, check it out, I brought a deer instead of a bear!

Oh, man. We recovered our wits and our breath as we continued on for what seemed like forever, and finally around dusk the canyon opened out and it wasn't much longer before we were at the highway. I rode Joe on the shoulder and we had another interminable stretch before finally Grouse Creek was on our right, and when I went to turn Joe onto the property, he refused—he was on autopilot, worn out and just plodding ahead, not even realizing where we were.

I estimated that ride at 26 miles. I gave Joe a good rub-down, paying special attention to his back and legs. He got a double ration of grain and 2 flakes of the local nutritious grass hay. Later that evening I went back to the barn and let him out into the big pasture, where he could roll and wander and eat the fresh grass and tell all his buddies what we did. That was the longest ride we took in the 9 years I had Joe.

The old Meadow Mountain Ski Lodge, which we used as our bunkhouse, had 4 levels including one that was partially below ground. As mentioned previously, on warm summer days and even nights, lots of windows and doors were left open. One night I was in the kitchen when I heard a commotion below. I went down the stairs, opened one of the doors and there was Ken, one of our wranglers, swinging his jacket trying to swat down a wayward bat. I yelled at him to stop and get out, which he did reluctantly, and then I bellowed for Claire, who I knew was down the hall in our shared room. When she came in, I pointed out the bat, which was now clinging to one of the ceiling beams, and asked her to stay there, keep the door closed and not let anyone else in, while I went to find something to trap the bat in so I could let it free outdoors. She agreed and I went out, passing Tedward on his way down the stairs to check out the action. I soon got hold of a tennis racket and a large paper bag, and when I neared the room again there was an explosion of noise—Tedward's loud, frantic barking, coupled with what sounded like a teakettle gone berserk.

When I opened the door, Claire was writhing on the floor, both hands to her head, screaming like a blonde in a Hitchcock movie. The bat was fluttering around, probably scared out of its wits. I yelled at Tedward and Claire both to get out of there, and locked the door. The bat landed on the same beam, I waited a minute or so and then stood on the bunk and nudged it into the bag with the racket. When I stood halfway up the outside steps and opened the bag, the bat flew out and was briefly silhouetted against the full moon, which had just risen over the peaks. When I asked Claire later why she was on the floor screaming, she said, "I don't know, it started flying around and I just freaked out." I made a mental note: no more bat-sitting for Claire.

We had a wrangler named Brick working for us in August and

September that year. Not your typical cowboy type, but capable with horses and people both, and a very nice guy. He and I were sitting on a hay bale between the lodge and the barn one evening, and at a little distance I pointed out something I thought was odd. It looked like a small section of the dried grasses was moving on its own. We both realized what it was at the same time: a badger! As it trotted along, its flowing coat moved with the motion, and matched the waving grass in color. I was glad to see my second wild badger, and to know that this one stood a good chance of living out its life, unlike the one in Wyoming.

One other little impromptu prank I pulled on Chris. I was picking up a manure pile on one side of the barn, and Chris was sitting on the bench that ran along the front, across from the reservation booth. When I stepped up onto the boardwalk with the shovel completely filled with steaming horseshit, Chris's head was turned away from me, and inspiration struck. I veered close to him and skimmed the edge of the shovel only a couple of inches from his chest as I carried it past. When he got a whiff of the pungent aroma, he jerked his head down to look and then quickly up and back, exhaling with disgust, but he couldn't move until I passed. It only took a second, but it's one of those precious little moments that will hopefully stay engraved on my memory forever.

Chapter 22

Tedward and Joe and I spent the winter of '80—'81 near Edwards, Colorado, which wasn't all that far from Grouse Creek. (The previous winter Tedward and I were in California, with Joe hanging out at Bob's in Lyons once again.) I boarded Joe at Stevenson's ranch, which was about a quarter mile from a trailer that Chris and Claire rented, and Tedward and I took the spare room. Chris had an elderly Irish Setter named Candy that had belonged to his family since she was a pup, and she lived in the trailer with us, usually sleeping on my bed. Tedward and Candy cordially disliked one another. I suspected this, although there had been no overt display of animosity for many weeks, until one evening when I saw Candy at her food dish and Tedward close by. They were looking into each other's eyes from a distance of about 8 inches, heads lowered close to the dish. I could hear low growling. This was amusing because Tedward so rarely came into any kind of conflict, subtle or otherwise, with other dogs. I cleared my throat in a particular way which Tedward knew well, and he suddenly found something interesting to sniff a little distance away.

He had one other unusual encounter, with a large malamute that lived a few trailers up the hill. I heard a burst of ugly snarling and when I opened the door, Tedward barreled in looking upset. He had a nasty gash on his abdomen, that went through all the layers of skin, but luckily not nicking the peritoneum. It was going to need a vet to stitch it, and it wasn't easy to find one, as it was the beginning of Thanksgiving weekend. Finally Dr. Parks, who was on his way out the door to go skiing, agreed to do it, and I remember holding Tedward's leg up for him when his assistant fainted and fell against the wall in a sitting position. I think that was the only wound Tedward ever got from another dog.

The total for his first 3 years of life: one coyote bite (from the Piney Lake coyote), one skunk spraying, and one dog bite. Considering the adventurous life he led, that wasn't too bad.

The next spring, I knew the time was getting close to say good-bye to old Joe. He had osteoarthritis in one knee so bad it was getting hard for him to get up off the ground after sleeping. I made the arrangements, feeling like I was closing an important chapter in my life, as I couldn't see getting another horse for awhile. Tedward and I headed over the mountains to Boulder, and my sister's house. I worked for a few months in an office, something pretty foreign to me, then and now. But in October I did a 3-week mule deer study on NCAR's property (National Center for Atmospheric Research). Tedward had to stay home for this little adventure. I sat on a rock (a "glacial erratic", brought down and deposited by a glacier eons before) with my binoculars and a sack lunch, and watched the deer and took notes on their behavior. It was eye-opening. I had no idea they played with each other so much. This herd was semi-habituated to humans, as hikers sometimes walked through this area, which was right at the base of the mountains. They soon got used to my presence and I could literally follow even the large bucks right up the trail, sitting within 20 feet when they lay down in the shade to chew their cuds. I was hoping to see some mating activity, but it was a little early in the year. I did see the bucks thrashing their antlers in the brush and polishing them against tree trunks. All the deer looked in the peak of health and fitness, even the one I called Grandpa, who had 13 points on one side and 12 on the other.

When I returned home in the late afternoons, Tedward and I walked to a nearby empty lot that had been taken over by prairie dogs. His Highness amused himself zig-zagging at high speed after them, similar to his antics at the Grouse Creek ground squirrel colony. For entertainment at dusk, we would sometimes walk through a stand of cottonwoods to stand on the creek bank behind the house, luring bats by loosely wrapping a bandanna around a rock, then lobbing it in the air. The bandanna would become disengaged, and its fluttering motion would draw the bats in close, as it resembled the movement of insect wings. We could hear the squeaking of their sonar as the bats zoomed around us. I think Chris was visiting us once when I showed him this technique—or maybe he's the one that showed it to me. (Easy, I'm in the springtime of my senility.)

We had some ridiculous wind in January, 1982. "Chinook winds", they were called, and they came down off the front range and blasted onto the plains at speeds of up to 150 mph. I was taking the bus home from the office, and I had to walk for about a quarter of a mile per- pendicular to the wind. Everybody on the sidewalk was leaned over, trudging along, until suddenly it would let up for a few seconds, and then we all staggered around like drunken sailors. Sometime after I got home, about 10 power poles snapped off 20 feet from their bases, and fell right into the street, making an incredible racket. Luckily no one got hurt.

That about sums up the excitement for that winter. In March, we boarded a plane and flew to Seattle, and my cousin's house, where Tedward met up with some old friends.

Chapter 23

My cousin had a 3-month-old litter of wire-haired dachshund puppies, and I realized how much Tedward had grown up, when I saw him in the kitchen surrounded by leaping pups with a look on his face that said, "Can somebody please get me out of here?". He was interested in them, but their constant pestering was too much to take, and he would stalk to the couch in the living room, jump up, and relax just out of their reach.

We were there about a week, and every morning and evening Tedward and I would take the canoe around the lake. When we would paddle close to swimming ducks, Tedward would be sitting bolt upright in the bow, trembling and whining with eagerness, and then finally he'd leap out and swim after them. I knew better than to try and haul him back aboard with no one else in the canoe to help steady it. After a strenuous (though fruitless) chase, Tedward would swim back to the beach, shake, roll vigorously with legs kicking, and flop down with a contented look on his face, satisfied that he'd done his duty.

There was a long driveway that curved through some huge fir trees, and the mailbox was at the end by the road. I volunteered to take Tedward for a walk and get the mail, and my cousin warned me that her neighbors had German Shepherds that often roamed their unfenced property. We set out and Tedward proceeded to mark most of the prominent bushes and tree trunks along the way. I was enjoying the sight of the sunlight streaming through the branches and the sound of the twittering birds, when about 50 yards in front of us 3 large dogs stepped out of the trees and looked our way.

All were magnificent specimens. They were the long-haired type of German Shepherds, and this added to my impression that each one was at least the size of an Irish Wolfhound and a St. Bernard combined. Tedward stopped in his tracks, staring, and then took off toward them at a gallop, roaring and bellowing at the top of his lungs. I tried to call him back, but he was on a mission. The shepherds stepped onto the pavement and waited; I covered my eyes. The thought flew through my mind that maybe my cousin, being a veterinarian, would give me a discount on his treatment, if he lived.

When the caterwauling stopped, I peeked through my fingers. Tedward, looking tiny, stood nose to nose with all 3 of the massive creatures, and all tails were wagging. A second later they were all frisking in the driveway, like they were so happy to see each other—as if they had known each other before. I was amazed. It had totally looked like Tedward was acting in an aggressive manner, but obviously that was not the case, and thank heavens the other dogs knew it.

When we headed back to the San Francisco bay area, life became disturbingly normal. There were trips to the beach, and parks to go to and socialize with other dogs, and hills and trails to explore, but it was all somehow very ordinary. It was a still a good life for Tedward, but compared to the years just passed, I thought it was unspeakably dull. He was now in his middle years, and able to handle almost any situation that it was possible to encounter. But there was no showcase for his skills and talents, no real challenges. Tedward seemed as happy as ever, thankfully.

The 80's were dull for many people, I've heard. When I took some law enforcement classes at De Anza College, Tedward came with me. He liked the gun class best, (the classroom sessions, not the range) because he could wander the room, getting and giving attention where needed, without restraint. He would never force himself on anyone. If they weren't interested in saying hello, he'd ease on down the row of seats. He seemed to sense just how much a person wanted to interact, and in what way. When he finished cruising the room, he'd come back to lie at my feet.

One day our teacher, a Sunnyvale cop, asked to use my Smith and Wesson to show something to the class. When he lifted it so the class could see, he kind of frowned, squinted his eyes and reached out and plucked something from one of the chambers, and held it up. "Is this a dog hair?" he asked innocently, and the class, mostly guys, started snickering and laughing. The smart alec behind me said, "Yeah, she pistol-whips her dog every night."

The years went by, people and animals came and went, but Tedward and I endured. I was working as a veterinary technician when I happened on a collie/shepherd pup that needed a home. Tedward was 10 years old when I added Figi to our family. He truly got his comeuppance for all the grief he dished out to older dogs when he was a pup. But he knew how to put the kibosh on Figi's shenanigans if she got to be too much for him. He did put up with alot of harassment though. I'd occasionally catch them being sweet to each other, sleeping right next to each other, drinking water at the same time, etc. They made a great pair, even though Tedward couldn't keep up with her in her mad dashes around the yard.

I was walking them in a city park one day, and there was a pit bull a little distance away, standing on a blanket with his human family nearby. He was looking at my dogs, and Tedward was interested in him and wanted to go over there. He was getting pretty creaky by then, and I looked at the other dog's powerful build, and I said "Sorry, boy, not this time." I just wasn't willing to take the chance, much as I trusted his ability to gauge other dogs' intentions. He gave me a look of pure reproach. I felt bad, but mostly because it really came home to me then how old my buddy was getting.

Chapter 24

I thought back to all the times in his life that Tedward entertained people and dogs and other animals, and what a great pal he was to travel with and explore the deserts and mountains and seashore. It was pretty painful to think of it all coming to an end. But he had one more bit of service to give, courtesy of the Furry Friends Foundation.

I'm not sure if they're still in existence, but this was a group of people and their "therapy dogs", that went to visit hospitals and nursing homes, to bring a little joy to the people there. Tedward passed the qualifying test with flying colors, and he soon showed that he was perfect for the job. He radiated gentleness and love to staff and patients alike. There was a teenage girl in the burn unit of one hospital that really took to him. He would sit by her wheelchair, resting his head on her knee as she stroked him gently, over and over. The feeble old ladies in the nursing homes were my favorite. It was wonderful to watch Tedward slowly approach and gaze upwards with his soulful brown eyes, and see a trembling hand reach out to touch him. He also had a strangely calming effect on the other dogs. I chuckled inwardly, remembering him running with the coyotes and chasing horses and making mischief all over the place. It was beautiful to watch him share his gentle and affectionate nature with these sick and elderly people.

If you're thinking I'm going to give you a detailed death scene, you're about to be disappointed. I saw a bumper sticker once that said, "Death Sucks"—that about sums up my feelings about it: the less said, the better.

When he was 15, Tedward started falling down. Then one day when he fell, he couldn't or wouldn't get up. Those eloquent eyes sent us the message: "It's time." With a little help from the vet, Tedward began his journey to the Great Beyond. I don't claim to know where or what that is, but I do know this: I'd very much like to meet up with him again, and if he's not where I'm going, then I don't want to go there.

Epilogue

Tedward did have one more coyote contact during his golden years, at Rancho San Antonio Park in Los Altos, California. I believe he was about 12 years old then. We spotted a coyote about 50 yards away at the edge of some brush, and Tedward started whining and carrying on. I looked around for rangers, saw none, and unhooked his leash. He dashed down the hill and streaked across the dry meadow toward the coyote, who stood his ground, watching him come. When Tedward screeched to a halt about 15 feet away, the coyote dropped his head down, opened his jaw wide, humped his back and began to dance nimbly to and fro in the classic defensive/aggressive posture. It was plain to see that Tedward couldn't understand the coyote's reluctance to say hello. I felt for him as I shouted for him to come back, and he came toward me, his body language reflecting his disappointment. Just then I saw a person approaching from my right. Yep, a ranger, and yes, we got a ticket. Figures it would be in California. (I'm always amused at people who think California is such a free-and-easy, anything-goes sort of place. It isn't.)

In case you think I'm advocating dogs and coyotes interacting, nothing could be further from the truth. To say that that's a risky proposition is an understatement. Tedward's situation was unusual. His success with the Grouse Creek pack was due to his unique personality, size, speed, overall strength, intelligence, the coyotes' personalities, and most of all, me and Joe coming to his rescue at opportune times.

So when you're out walking with your dog on a beautiful trail, and the coyotes start to sing, and your dog starts to whine and prance and act like he wants to join them, fix him with your best alpha stare and firmly say, "Don't do it!" And then feel free to add what I say now to my dogs: "Who do you think you are—Tedward?"

THE END

Horseshoe Park, Rocky Mountain National Park. See the bighorns?

Chapter Notes

Chapter 1: *Chris reminded me of what I'd told him about the tail end of the Meadow Mountain trip years ago: On the last night, we were down at the campground near the trailhead, and as I was setting up our site, I saw a hay wagon with a bunch of old ladies in it drawn by 2 horses, coming up the dirt road. I had tethered Joe with a stout rope to a tree near the stream, and I tied Nikki up to another tree, just in case. Tedward I trusted to stick around and behave himself, more or less. The ladies were being helped off the wagon and gathering around the stone grill where their tour leader was building a fire, and soon they were laying out dishes and containers for what looked to be a prodigious feast. I got my fire going and began heating the water for macaroni and cheese, after giving Joe his grain and Nikki and Tedward their first course of Kibbles and Bits. I had just added the noodles when I heard Joe's hooves clattering on the rocks by the water, and when I turned to look, I saw he had one leg tangled in his rope and was starting to panic. I jumped up and rushed over, but before I could get close, Joe snapped the rope with his thrashing and took off running right toward the old ladies! I froze in horror, knowing I couldn't reach them in time to do anything, but thankfully Joe swerved to avoid them and rushed by the group without trampling anyone. I think I aged a year in those few seconds. I apologized to the people as I went to catch him, calmed him down, and tied him much farther away. Gawd. When I sat back down near the fire, I apparently bumped something because right then my macaroni and cheese fell upside down right into the fire. Man was I hungry. Well, maybe I had a granola bar in my pack. Then I heard a voice nearby say,

"Excuse me dear, would you like some dinner?" There was a blue-haired oldster holding a plate heaped, I say heaped, with food. Hot dog, hamburger, potato salad, pickles, chips, etc. I looked up at her like the angel she was, and asked if she knew my dinner had just fallen in the fire, to which she replied in the negative. I said, "I hope my horse didn't scare you too badly." She said, "Oh no, it's fine dear—a little excitement at our age is good for us!"

Chapter 2: *I cooked dinner a couple of times for the Scottish gentleman, and one time when we were just sitting down to eat a car pulled up to his shop. I was surprised when he grabbed his jacket and prepared to head out the door. I said, "It's late, are you going to open the shop now?" and he said, "Oh yes!" I was shaking my head as he went out, and I watched through the window of his trailer as he greeted the people and unlocked the door, ushering them in. Just as he got to the threshold he leaned back, saw me watching, and rubbed his thumb and fingers together in the universal symbol for money, and his face broke out in a grin.

Chapter 3: *Thanks to Dave, we do have one picture!

Chapter 6: *I nicknamed her "Circus Dog" because of the way she would balance on her hind legs and turn circles. Cute little cuss.

Chapter 10: *We have reconnected with Dave, and he will get his chance to be bothered by my current dog, Poppy, this October when we have our Wranglers' Reunion.

Chapter 12: *That same veterinarian was willing to try one more time to give Joe his shots, but he would only do it if we put him—Joe, not the vet—in one of the narrow holding chutes at the rodeo grounds. We got him in there and when Joe realized what was happening he was pretty ticked off, but luckily he wasn't foolish enough to have a hissy fit while pinned in the chute.

**I remember one other time I chased a herd of elk, on some property adjacent to Foothills Ranch, in company with the daughter of the ranch owner. The sound of the galloping hooves, the enthusiasm of Joe as he raced after the sprinting herd, the swirling dust, and the fading light illuminating the elks' antlers made for a memorable few minutes.

Chapter 13: *Jeff and Flossie both will get to see how creatively I've "augmented" my former shape, at the Wranglers' Reunion.

Chapter 15: *Kathy was a charming and sophisticated young lady with impeccable manners—which made her crazy, oddball antics especially hilarious. She was the star of our show during those times in Estes Park, and we are all very sorry she had to leave this earth so soon.

Chapter 16: *Chris told me recently that he was irritated because I would make so much noise to keep the bears away that everything else stayed away too. No wonder we only saw one caribou, instead of a whole herd!

**Chris has a completely different memory of our first crossing of the McKinley River. He said the staff he cut was too green, and it started to bow under the pressure he was putting on it when we were in a really deep channel. He said the water was past his waist, and almost up to my armpits, and that we were stuck—unable to move forward—for several minutes. I do not remember this at all. I asked him how we got out of it, and he said he just kept struggling to move his right foot and finally it moved an inch, then another, and he was able to step with his left a little, and since he was breaking the force of the current for me, I was able to follow. I was close be-hind him, holding on to his pack frame, as there was no rope tied to his pack like on the second crossing. Wow. I wonder if it was so scary I just blanked it totally from my memory. He reminded me after the trip was over what the rangers had told us: that every year, people die in that river.

Acknowledgements

First thanks go to Susan, my good friend since 1975, who not only brought Tedward to me, but has had my back through thick and thin, and has kept a hard copy of all my pages in case of disaster. Thank you to Jamie, my publishing consultant, and the others at Outskirts Press, for putting up with an old lady whose computer knowledge contains massive gaps, and whose impatience is legendary. Thank you to Andrew, editor, for challenging me to write for the Pawhuska Oklahoma Nature Conservancy Tallgrass Prairie Preserve Docent Newsletter (try saying that 5 times fast), and for publishing 4 of my coyote articles and one of my kids' stories, which led me to write this book. Thanks to my San Diego buddy Kareen Novak, for sharing her experience of publishing her children's story, "The Seal's Gift". Thank you to my sister Teddy for being encouraging and supportive in multiple ways, and for allowing Tedward to use her name as his own during his puppyhood. Thanks to Dave, who actually sounded happy to hear from me, and wants to have a "Wrangler's Reunion" at his house. (I wonder if he realizes what he's in for; that party alone could provide enough material for a book.) Thank you to Jeff—yes, the Indiana scalawag—and Flossie, and Beth and Karen, for playing such huge parts during those wonderful years, and to Kathy, who, we were saddened to learn, passed away in 2009, and who is now hopefully keeping Tedward and Joe company until we all end up at the same awesome place.

Chris, what can I say. You've probably put up with more of my shenanigans than anyone. In spite of my severe shortcomings—liking Arabian horses, for instance—and many instances of bad behavior—such as ditching you in Jackson, buzzing you with a shovelful of manure, and embarrassing you countless times in restaurants with my loud cackling, you continue to be my friend. This could be in part because I've been willing to put up with your nicknames and beach jokes all these years. For those of you unfamiliar with this rather low brand of humor, here's an example of Chris's latest effort: "Man, it must be hard to relax on the beach when all those Santa Cruz animal lovers are constantly trying to push you back in the water", followed by the old hee-haw. It's sad when one is the only person laughing at his own jokes. So here's to you, pardner, and I hope you'll think of this book as my way of attempting to follow your oft-repeated instructions to "Stay on top."

Caryl Pearson
August 2014, Santa Cruz, CA

CPSIA information can be obtained
at www.ICGtesting.com
Printed in the USA
LVOW02s1500190916

505259LV00011B/56/P